SOCIAL SECURITY LAW

by
Margaret C. Jasper, Esq.

Oceana's Legal Almanac Series:
Law for the Layperson

1999
Oceana Publications, Inc.
Dobbs Ferry, N.Y.

Information contained in this work has been obtained by Oceana Publications from sources believed to be reliable. However, neither the Publisher nor its authors guarantee the accuracy or completeness of any information published herein, and neither Oceana nor its authors shall be responsible for any errors, omissions or damages arising from the use of this information. This work is published with the understanding that Oceana and its authors are supplying information, but are not attempting to render legal or other professional services. If such services are required, the assistance of an appropriate professional should be sought.

You may order this or any other Oceana publications by visiting Oceana's Web Site at http://www.oceanalaw.com

Library of Congress Cataloging-in-Publication Data

Jasper, Margaret C.
    Social security law / by Margaret C. Jasper.
        p. cm.—(Oceana's legal almanac series.   Law for the layperson)
    Includes bibliographical references.
    ISBN 0-379-11332-5 (alk. paper)
    1. Old age pensions—Law and legislation—United States Popular works. 2. Disability retirement—Law and legislation—United States Popular works. I. Title. II. Series.
KF3650.J37 1999
344.73'023—dc21   99-20494
                                          CIP

Oceana's Legal Almanac Series: Law for the Layperson
ISSN 1075-7376

Manufactured in the United States of America on acid-free paper.

$22.50   HRL-4926   7/21

To My Husband Chris

Your love and support
are my motivation and inspiration

-and-

In memory of my son, Jimmy

Other Volumes Available in the Series

For more information or to order call: 1-914-693-8100
or visit us at www.oceanalaw.com

ABOUT THE AUTHOR

MARGARET C. JASPER is an attorney engaged in the general practice of law in South Salem, New York, concentrating in the areas of personal injury and entertainment law. Ms. Jasper holds a Juris Doctor degree from Pace University School of Law, White Plains, New York, is a member of the New York and Connecticut bars, and is certified to practice before the United States District Courts for the Southern and Eastern Districts of New York, and the United States Supreme Court. Ms. Jasper has been appointed to the panel of arbitrators of the American Arbitration Association and the law guardian panel for the Family Court of the State of New York, is a member of the Association of Trial Lawyers of America, and is a New York State licensed real estate broker and member of the Westchester County Board of Realtors, operating as Jasper Real Estate, in South Salem, New York.

Ms. Jasper is the author and general editor of the following legal almanacs: Juvenile Justice and Children's Law; Marriage and Divorce; Estate Planning; The Law of Contracts; The Law of Dispute Resolution; Law for the Small Business Owner; The Law of Personal Injury; Real Estate Law for the Homeowner and Broker; Everyday Legal Forms; Dictionary of Selected Legal Terms; The Law of Medical Malpractice; The Law of Product Liability; The Law of No-Fault Insurance; The Law of Immigration; The Law of Libel and Slander; The Law of Buying and Selling; Elder Law; The Right to Die; AIDS Law; The Law of Obscenity and Pornography; The Law of Child Custody; The Law of Debt Collection; Consumer Rights Law; Bankruptcy Law for the Individual Debtor; Victim's Rights Law; Animal Rights Law; Workers' Compensation Law; Employee Rights in the Workplace; Probate Law; Environmental Law; Labor Law; The Americans with Disabilities Act; The Law of Capital Punishment; Education Law; The Law of Violence Against Women; Landlord-Tenant Law; Insurance Law; Religion and the Law; Commercial Law; and Motor Vehicle Law.

TABLE OF CONTENTS

APPENDICES

INTRODUCTION

A fact of life which society cannot ignore is the financial dependence of its aging population. The social security system is concerned with providing people with economic security, particularly when they reach the age where they are no longer able to work to support themselves, or are otherwise disabled and unable to earn a living.

The traditional sources of economic security include one's assets; income and pension; family resources; and charitable organizations. Unfortunately, one or more of these sources of economic security are not always available to everyone in need, and people look to their government for assistance.

The social security system is a statutory creation. The Social Security Act of 1934 was passed primarily to provide a retirement pension program for senior citizens and assist disabled individuals. Over the past 60 years, the social security system has become an essential component of modern American life. It addresses the needs of those whose economic security is threatened by events such as unemployment, illness, disability, death, and old age.

One in seven Americans receives some type of social security benefit. More than 90 percent of all workers are in jobs covered by social security. In 1940, approximately 222,000 people received monthly social security benefits. Today, benefits are distributed to over 42 million Americans.

This almanac explores the history of the legislation and early administration of the social security system, and the manner in which the system is funded and wages are recorded. This almanac also discusses the establishment of the Social Security Administration, and the individual programs it administers, such as retirement pension benefits, medicare, supplemental security income, survivor benefits, and disability benefits, including eligibility and application information.

The Appendices provide sample forms and documents, and other pertinent information and data. The Glossary contains definitions of many of the terms used throughout the almanac.

CHAPTER 1:

HISTORY AND DEVELOPMENT
OF SOCIAL INSURANCE

The English Model

In the Middle Ages, European society recognized that economic security could be obtained by the formation of formal organizations which protected their members. The earliest of such organizations were the merchant and craftsmen guilds. These guilds were formed by individuals who had a common trade or business.

In addition to regulating production and employment, these organizations provided benefits—e.g., financial assistance and death benefits—to their members in time of need. These guilds evolved into what were known as fraternal organizations—forerunners of the modern trade unions—which began the practice of offering life insurance to members. Following the Industrial Revolution, these types of organizations flourished and, by the early 19th century, one in nine men belonged to such an organization. In fact, early American settlers continued the establishment of fraternal organizations in the American colonies.

The English "Poor Laws"

As the government stepped in and began to assume responsibility for its citizens' economic security, a series of *Poor Laws* were adopted to help the disadvantaged. The *English Poor Law of 1601* was the first statute which dealt with the government's responsibility to provide for the welfare of its people. Under this statute, taxes were assessed to fund relief programs which were locally controlled, and *almshouses* were founded to shelter the homeless.

Although the law acknowledged the government's responsibility for the needy, it was also considered harsh in that it viewed the poor as undesirables and treated them likewise. In addition, amongst the poor, there were distinctions made as to which individuals were deserving of aid and which individuals were ineligible.

American Colonies

When the English-speaking colonists arrived in America, they established *Poor Laws* similar to those they were accustomed to in England. The early colonial laws also used taxation as a means to fund the programs, which were again administered locally. The colonies also distinguished between poor persons who were deemed "worthy" of assistance, and those who were not eligible for relief.

As the colonies expanded, local control over financial aid to the poor became burdensome, and state assistance was sought. Through the 18th and 19th centuries, "almshouses" and "poorhouses" were instituted to shelter and provide relief to the indigent population. However, obtaining such relief was purposely made very difficult in order to discourage dependency on the state. For example, personal property could be forfeited, as well as the right to vote and freely move throughout society. In some cases, those receiving assistance were required to display certain markings on their clothing.

Distributing financial assistance outside of the poorhouses was frowned upon because the citizens did not want to encourage dependency on the state by making it easier to obtain help. However, operating the poorhouses became increasingly expensive, and some financial assistance outside of the poorhouse setting began to occur. Nevertheless, society sought to keep government assistance in this area to a bare minimum.

The Civil War Period

The Civil War resulted in hundreds of thousands of disabled veterans, widows and orphans. During that time, the dependent American population was proportionally the largest it has ever been in history. In response to this crisis, a pension program, with many similarities to our current social security system, was developed.

The first piece of legislation was passed in 1862, and provided pension benefits to soldiers who were disabled as a result of their military duty. Widows and orphans were eligible for pension benefits that their parent or spouse would have received had they been disabled. Nevertheless, former Confederate soldiers and their families were barred from receiving Civil War pensions.

By 1890, a military service connected disability was no longer required, thus any disabled Civil War veteran was eligible for benefits and, by 1906, Civil War pension benefits were extended to older Americans. Nevertheless, this forerunner of the modern social security system was not extended to the general population until much later.

The Industrial Revolution

The deterioration of the traditional sources of economic security in America was attributed to cultural and demographic changes which began with the Industrial Revolution. The Industrial Revolution transformed a largely agricultural society to a nation of industrial workers. Thus, individuals could no longer depend on their own hard work to put a meal on the table for their family, but were subject to conditions outside of their control, such as the possibility of unemployment.

In addition, the change from an agricultural society to an industrial society forced many Americans to move from farms to urban areas, and largely accounted for the subsequent disappearance of the extended family—i.e., a household which included grandparents and other relatives. The extended family was beneficial in that the family assumed financial responsibility for any members who became disabled or too old to work.

Another significant and related demographic change which developed was the increase in life expectancy due, in large part, to advances in public health care. As a result, there was a rapid growth in the elderly population, and there were no programs in place to address this growing need.

The Depression Era

In the 1920s, it was not just the wealthy who invested their fortunes in the stock market. There were many smaller investors who gambled their modest incomes in a system that promised them riches. When the stock market crashed on October 24, 1929, the economic security of millions of Americans disappeared overnight and America slipped into an economic Depression.

In the 1930s, America's economy was in crisis. Unemployment was at a record level, banks and businesses were failing, and the majority of the elderly population lived in poverty. Prior to the 1930s, there were virtually no state welfare pensions for the elderly. In response to changing demographics and the growing economic crisis, approximately 30 states passed some form of old-age welfare pension program by 1935. However, benefits under these programs were modest, eligibility was restricted based on income, and many of the programs were inadequately implemented.

There was a public outcry for a federal response to this growing problem, and a number of movements developed, each with a proposed pension scheme. President Herbert Hoover responded that the most effective way to combat economic insecurity was through voluntary relief. Hoover had enjoyed success in international relief efforts, before and after World War I, through the efforts of voluntary partnerships of government, business and private donations.

Hoover believed this kind of "volunteerism" would solve the problems of the Depression. Although he authorized some limited federal relief efforts, his main response to the Depression was to advocate these voluntary efforts. Unfortunately, voluntary charity proved impossible because the nation's wealth had been so profoundly diminished in the three years following the stock market crash.

The Concept of Social Insurance—The Roosevelt Administration

President Franklin D. Roosevelt introduced an economic security proposal based on social insurance rather than welfare assistance to address the permanent problem of economic security for the elderly. Social insurance programs had been successfully implemented in many European countries since the 19th century.

Social insurance endeavors to solve the problem of threatened economic security by pooling risk assets from a large social group and providing income to those members of the group whose economic security is imperiled, e.g., by unemployment, disability, or cessation of work due to old age.

Under Roosevelt's proposal, a work-related, contributory system would be created in which workers would provide for their own future economic security through taxes paid while employed. The Social Security program that was eventually adopted in late 1935 relied on this concept of "social insurance."

The Social Security Act of 1935

The Social Security Act was signed by President Roosevelt on August 14, 1935. Originally, the Social Security Act was named the Economic Security Act, but this title was changed during Congressional consideration of the bill. Taxes were collected for the first time in January 1937 and the first one-time lump-sum payments were made that same month.

One-time lump-sum payments were the only form of benefits paid during the start-up period beginning January 1937 through December 1939. The earliest reported recipient of a lump-sum benefit was a retired Cleveland motorman named Ernest Ackerman. Mr. Ackerman retired one day after the Social Security program began. During his one day of participation in the program, a nickel was withheld from Mr. Ackerman's pay for Social Security. Upon his retirement, Mr. Ackerman received a lump-sum payment of 17 cents.

Regular ongoing monthly benefits started in January 1940. On January 31, 1940, the first monthly Social Security retirement check was issued to

Ida May Fuller of Ludlow, Vermont, in the amount of $22.54. Miss Fuller died in January 1975 at the age of 100. During her 35 years as a beneficiary, she received over $22,000 in benefits.

Under the 1935 law, Social Security only paid retirement benefits to the primary worker. A 1939 change in the law added survivors benefits and benefits for the retiree's spouse and children. Disability benefits were added in 1956.

Organization of the Social Security Administration

The Social Security Act of 1935 established the three-member *Social Security Board* to administer the programs established by the Act, which included social security, unemployment compensation and various public assistance programs. The Board then established the *Bureau of Federal Old-Age Insurance*—subsequently renamed the *Bureau of Old-Age and Survivors Insurance*—as the agency responsible for administering social security benefits.

In 1946, the Social Security Board was abolished and the Social Security Administration (SSA) was established. In 1963, a Welfare Administration was established to administer the public assistance programs, leaving social security to the Social Security Administration and marking the end of the Bureau of Old-Age and Survivors Insurance.

The Social Security Board, and the subsequent Social Security Administration, were under the jurisdiction of the Federal Security Agency from 1939 to 1953, when the Department of Health, Education, and Welfare—subsequently renamed the *Department of Health and Human Services*—was established and designated the SSA's parent organization.

Throughout the 1980s and 1990s, there was growing bipartisan support for removing the SSA from under the Department of Health and Human Services, and establishing it as an independent agency. In 1994, the Social Security Independence and Program Improvements Act of 1994 (P.L. 103-296) was passed unanimously by Congress and, on August 14, 1994, President Bill Clinton signed the Act into law. The SSA now operates as an independent agency.

A directory of Social Security Administration Regional Offices is set forth at Appendix 1.

Modern Day Social Security

Social Security is now known as *Old Age, Survivors and Disability Insurance (OASDI)* under Title II of the Social Security Act. It is a national program created by Congress, which pays money to retirees, survivors of deceased workers, and people who have become disabled. Although there are a variety of benefits paid out under the social security program, social security commonly refers to money paid to older workers or retirees who have made contributions to the program from their earned income. Most employees are required to contribute, though some state and local government workers are exempt.

From the beginning, it was recognized that the provision of old-age annuities for some 30 to 40 million men and women was clearly a massive undertaking never before attempted by the Federal Government. Administratively, old-age insurance loomed up as the leviathan of the Social Security Act. Unlike unemployment compensation programs and public assistance programs, which are administered jointly by the Federal Government with assistance by the state governments, the administration of old-age insurance is a responsibility assumed by the Federal Government alone. Though consideration of state laws enters into one aspect of old-age insurance, administration of this program is comparatively simple. Most of its problems arise from its size.

The concept of "retirement" after a long period of working years was not always available to the elderly before the social security system was developed. When the Social Security retirement benefits program was instituted, it was not intended to provide a comfortable standard of living in retirement, but to supplement income, including personal savings and pension benefits. Unfortunately, many senior citizens are now trying to live out their retirement years dependent solely on their Social Security checks. This may be due to the fact that their former employment did not provide a pension, or because they did not save any money during their working years to supplement their social security income.

CHAPTER 2:

THE SOCIAL SECURITY NUMBER AND CARD

History of the Social Security Number

Following the enactment of the Social Security Act of 1935, the Social Security Board was faced with the enormous task of registering workers and employers so that they could begin earning credits toward old-age benefits by January 1, 1937.

The Social Security Board had to devise a system whereby each worker could be identified and connected with the wages reported by his or her employer so that there would be a complete and accurate record to use in order to compute the worker's benefits. Using names and addresses as a means of identification was ruled out because many thousands of workers had identical names, and addresses would only have short-term usage. Another means of positive identification was necessary.

It was finally decided that each covered individual would be assigned an account number, and personal information would be obtained for permanent association between the individual and the account number. This personal information, supplied by the worker when applying for an account number, included: name and address; employer's name and address at time of filing; age and date of birth; place of birth; father's full name; mother's maiden name; sex; color; and signature.

The assignment of a social security number (SSN) to each individual worker in covered employment was begun in November 1936. However, because the newly-formed Social Security Board did not have sufficient resources, they contracted with the U.S. Postal Service to accomplish the registration process.

The local post offices distributed the applications and assigned the social security numbers. The post offices then collected the completed forms and turned them over to the Social Security field offices located near major post office centers. The applications were forwarded to Baltimore, Maryland, where the social security numbers were registered and various employment records established. The process of issuing social security numbers is called *enumeration*.

With the assistance of the post offices, over 30 million social security numbers were issued through this early registration procedure. In addition, more than 2.6 million identification numbers were assigned to employers. By June 30, 1937, the Social Security Board had established 151 field offices and was able to take over the responsibility of assigning social security numbers. By the end of March 1938, applications for account numbers totaled more than 38 million.

Today the issuance of social security numbers is essentially a fully automated process. This process is known as the *Automated Enumeration Screening Process.* The field offices receive the applications, verify the identity proofs, and electronically transmit the information from the application to the Central Office for assignment of a number. In the Central Office the information is checked by computer against information already on file to determine whether the application duplicates an earlier application. If so, a duplicate card is issued. Otherwise, unless there are discrepancies, a new social security number is assigned and a new card is issued.

The original application, which is retained for a short period of time in the field office, is later sent to a records center in Pennsylvania for microfilming and filing. The original document is destroyed once the microfilm has been made. If the original document is needed for a signature verification or fraud investigation, a microprint is produced from the film.

According to the Social Security Administration, approximately 381 million social security numbers have been assigned as of 1996.

A table of total social security numbers issued by calendar year (1936-1996) is set forth at Appendix 2.

Meaning of the Social Security Account Number

The social security account number is composed of nine digits, divided into three sections. The first three digits specify a geographical area, the next two indicate a group, and the remaining four specify an individual serial number. The United States, Alaska, and Hawaii are divided into approximately 380 different administrative areas, each with a different number.

The area number which an individual's account bears is determined by the area in which he resided at the time he registered. Generally, area numbers were assigned beginning in the northeast and moving westward. Thus, people on the east coast have the lowest numbers and those on the west coast have the highest numbers.

A table listing social security area numbers by geographical region is set forth at Appendix 3.

The group number, indicated by the fourth and fifth digits, was determined by the procedure of issuing numbers in groups of 10,000 to post offices for assignment at the beginning of the enumeration. The group number no longer has any significance. The serial number is determined by the order, within area and group, in which numbers are assigned.

Because the 9-digit social security number allows for about 1 billion possible combinations, and only 390 million have been issued to date, the Social Security Administration does not expect to have to recycle old numbers for quite some time. Thus, when an individual dies, their number is not reissued to another person. The decedent's social security number is simply removed form the active files and is not reused.

History of the Social Security Card

Following the enactment of the Social Security Act of 1935, the Social Security Board considered a number of options in devising a social security identification card before it settled on the paper card that has been in existence for most of the past 50 years.

An initial proposal was to issue each worker a small metal plate upon which his or her name and number would be embossed, similar to a charge plate. This proposal had a number of advantages. The plate would be durable, and could be attached to a key ring to prevent loss. Employers could use its imprint to ensure an accurate record of the worker's social security number.

Nevertheless, this proposal was ultimately rejected because the plates could not be prepared in time to ensure completion of the initial enumeration by January 1, 1937. There was also public dissatisfaction in that the metal plates looked too much like military "dog tags" and were considered by many to signal excessive uniformity. The use of fingerprints to identify individuals for social security purposes was also rejected because there was such a strong association in the public mind between fingerprinting and criminality.

The Social Security Board also considered the possibility of attaching the worker's photograph to the card. However, this plan was discarded because it was too costly for the Government to photograph all workers. The Board also concluded that photographs would have to be updated over time.

In recent years, Congress has become concerned about the privacy of social security numbers due to their increasing use for non-social security related purposes, thus increasing the possibility of fraud. Most recently, the Social Security Amendments of 1983 (Public Law 98-21) required that the social security card be made of banknote paper and, to the extent practicable, be counterfeit-proof. Beginning with cards issued on October 31, 1983, all new and replacement cards have met these criteria, marking the first substantial physical change in the card's appearance in 47 years.

Applying for a Social Security Card

If an individual needs to replace a lost Social Security card, change the name shown on their card, or request a new card, they must complete an Application for a Social Security Card (SSA Form SS-5).

In addition to completing Form SS-5, the applicant must provide originals or certified copies of certain documents, as set forth below.

Replacement Social Security Card

To obtain a replacement card, the applicant generally needs only one identifying document. The replacement card will have the same social security number as the original card. The following documents are accepted by the SSA as proof of identity:

1. Driver's license;
2. Marriage or divorce record;
3. Military records;
4. Employer ID card;
5. Adoption record;
6. Insurance policy;
7. Passport;
8. Health Insurance card (but not a Medicare card); or
9. School ID card.

Amended Social Security Card

To change the name on a social security card, the applicant needs documentation that shows their old name and their new name. The new card will show the new name but will have the same number as the original card.

New Social Security Card

To obtain a new social security card, the applicant will need to provide documents that show their age, citizenship or lawful alien status, and proof of identity as set forth above. Applicants age 18 or over who have never had a social security number must go to a Social Security office in person to apply. Applicants who were born outside the United States must also show proof of citizenship or lawful alien status.

A copy of an Application for a Social Security Card (SSA Form SS-5) is attached at Appendix 4.

Social Security Number as Identification

The initial registration only assigned social security numbers to adults who were working in covered employment. Over the years, the social security number has become widely used for purposes not associated with the social security program. Many governments, schools, businesses, and financial institutions use an individual's social security number for client identification and record-keeping purposes.

As a result, the average age of applicants has dropped considerably. Currently, about 94 percent of all applicants are under age 22; 74 percent are under age 15; and 41 percent are under age 5, the majority of which are under age 2.

Although obtaining a social security number for a newborn is strictly voluntary, the Social Security Administration urges parents to obtain a social security number for their newborns at birth for a number of reasons. For example, any child claimed on a taxpayer's income tax return must have a social security number. In addition, children generally need their own social security number if a bank account will be opened for them, or savings bonds purchased for them. Social security numbers for children may also be needed to obtain medical coverage or apply for various types of government services.

A parent may request a social security number for a newborn at the time the hospital representative requests information for the baby's birth certificate, and a social security card will be processed. If the social security number is not requested at the hospital, one may be obtained later by contacting the local Social Security office and filing the necessary papers.

Privacy of Social Security Records

The Social Security Administration guarantees the privacy of one's social security records unless: (i) disclosure to another agency is required by law; or (ii) the information is needed to conduct Social Security or other government health or welfare programs.

If a business requests your social security number, you may refuse to give it to them. However, refusal may mean that the business will not provide the service offered. For example, an individual may apply for a store credit card. In that connection, the credit grantor may request the applicant's social security number. If the applicant refuses to supply their social security number, the credit grantor may refuse to issue the credit card.

If a business requests your social security number, you should inquire as to: (i) why it is needed; (ii) how it is going to be used; (iii) what law, if any, requires you to supply your social security number; and (iv) the consequences if you refuse to supply your social security number.

Misuse of a Social Security Number

It is against the law to use someone else's Social Security number, or to give false information when applying for a number. It is also illegal to alter, buy or sell Social Security cards. Anyone convicted of these crimes is subject to fines and/or imprisonment.

The misuse of a person's social security number can cause a number of problems for the victim. For example, an individual may misuse someone's social security number to obtain credit. Thus, it is important to protect both your social security number and card. If you suspect that someone is misusing your social security number, you should report it to the Office of Inspector General hotline at 1-800-269-0271.

Under certain circumstances, the Social Security Administration will assign a new social security number to a person who can document that they have been victimized and disadvantaged by the misuse of their social security number by another. In addition, in 1998, Vice President Gore announced a new policy allowing victims of domestic violence to change their social security number without proof that the abuser had misused their social security number.

Chronology of Legislation Affecting the Use of the Social Security Number (1935–1998)

In 1935, The Social Security Act (P.L. 74-271) was enacted. Although it did not expressly mention the use of social security numbers, it authorized the creation of some type of record-keeping scheme.

In 1936, Treasury Decision 4704 required the issuance of an account number to each employee covered by the Social Security program.

In 1943, Executive Order 9397 required: (i) all Federal components to use the social security number "exclusively" whenever the component found it advisable to set up a new identification system for individuals; and

(ii) the Social Security Board to cooperate with Federal uses of the number by issuing and verifying numbers for other Federal agencies.

In 1961, the Civil Service Commission adopted the SSN as an official Federal employee identifier.

In 1961, the Internal Revenue Code Amendments (P.L. 87-397) required each taxpayer to furnish identifying number for tax reporting.

In 1962, the Internal Revenue Service adopted the social security number as its official taxpayer identification number.

In 1964, the Treasury Department, via internal policy, required buyers of Series H savings bonds to provide their social security numbers.

In 1965, the Internal Revenue Amendments (P.L. 89-384) enacted Medicare. It became necessary for most individuals age 65 and older to have a social security number.

In 1966, the Veterans Administration began to use the social security number as the hospital admissions number and for patient record-keeping.

In 1967, the Department of Defense adopted the social security number in lieu of the military service number for identifying Armed Forces personnel.

In 1970, the Bank Records and Foreign Transactions Act (P.L. 91-508) required all banks, savings and loan associations, credit unions, and brokers/dealers in securities to obtain the social security numbers of all of their customers. Also, financial institutions were required to file a report with the IRS, including the social security number of the customer, for any transaction involving more than $10,000.

In 1971, an SSA task force report was published which proposed that the SSA take a "cautious and conservative" position toward social security number use and do nothing to promote the use of the social security number as an identifier. The report also recommended that the SSA use mass social security number enumeration in schools as a long-range, cost-effective approach to tightening up the social security number system, and consider cooperating with specific health, education and welfare uses of the social security number by State, local, and other nonprofit organizations.

In 1972, the Social Security Amendments of 1972 (P.L. 92-603): (i) required the SSA to issue social security numbers to all legally admitted aliens upon entry, and to anyone receiving or applying for any benefit paid for by Federal funds; (ii) required the SSA to obtain evidence to establish age, citizenship, or alien status and identity; and (iii) authorized the SSA to enumerate children at the time they first entered school.

In 1973, buyers of series E savings bonds were required by the Treasury Department to provide their social security numbers.

In 1973, a report of the HEW Secretary's Advisory Committee on Automated Personal Data System concluded that the adoption of a universal identifier by this country was not desirable; and also found that the social security number was not suitable for such a purpose as it does not meet the criteria of a universal identifier that distinguishes a person from all others.

In 1974, the Privacy Act (P.L. 93-579) was enacted, effective September 27, 1975, to limit governmental use of the social security number and: (i) provided that no State or local government agency may withhold a benefit from a person simply because the individual refuses to furnish his or her social security number; and (ii) required that Federal, State and local agencies which request an individual to disclose his or her social security number inform the individual if disclosure was mandatory or voluntary.

In 1975, the Social Services Amendments of 1974 (P.L. 93-647) provided that: (i) disclosure of an individual's social security number is a condition of eligibility for AFDC benefits; and (ii) the Office of Child Support Enforcement Parent Locator Service may require disclosure of limited information, including social security number and whereabouts, contained in SSA records.

In 1976, under the Tax Reform Act of 1976 (P.L. 94-455), amendments were made to the Social Security Act to: (i) allow use by the States of the social security number in the administration of any tax, general public assistance, driver's license or motor vehicle registration law within their jurisdiction and to authorize the States to require individuals affected by such laws to furnish their social security numbers to the States; (ii) make misuse of the social security number for any purpose a violation of the Social Security Act; (iii) make disclosure or compelling disclosure of the social security number of any person a violation of the Social Security Act; and (iv) amend section 6109 of the Internal Revenue Code to provide that the social security number be used as the tax identification number (TIN) for all tax purposes. While the Treasury Department had been using the social security number as the TIN by regulation since 1962, this law codified that requirement.

In 1976, the Federal Advisory Committee on False Identification: (i) recommended that penalties for misuse should be increased and evidence requirements tightened; and (ii) rejected the idea of a national identifier and would not consider the social security number for such a purpose.

In 1977, the Food Stamp Act of 1977 (P.L. 96-58) required disclosure of social security numbers of all household members as a condition of eligibility for participation in the food stamp program.

In 1977, a Privacy Protection Study Commission recommended that: (i) no steps be taken towards developing a standard, universal label for individuals until safeguards and policies regarding permissible uses and disclosures were proven effective; and (ii) Executive Order 9397 be amended so that Federal agencies could no longer use it as legal authority to require disclosure of an individual's social security number. However, no action was taken.

In 1978, the SSA required evidence of age, citizenship, and identity of all social security number applicants.

In 1981, the Omnibus Budget Reconciliation Act of 1981 (P.L. 97-35) required the disclosure of the social security numbers of all adult members in the household of children applying to the school lunch program.

In 1981, under the Social Security Benefits Act (P.L. 97-123): (i) Section 4 added alteration and forgery of a Social Security card to the list of prohibited acts and increased the penalties for such acts; and (ii) Section 6 required any Federal, State or local government agency to furnish the name and social security number of prisoners convicted of a felony to the Secretary of Health and Human Services, to enforce suspension of disability benefits to certain imprisoned felons.

In 1981, the Department of Defense Authorization Act (P.L. 97-86) required disclosure of the social security numbers to the Selective Service System of all individuals required to register for the draft.

In 1982, the Debt Collection Act (P.L. 97-365) required that all applicants for loans under any Federal loan program furnish their social security numbers to the agency supplying the loan.

In 1982, all social security cards issued to legal aliens not authorized to work within the United States were annotated "not valid for employment" beginning in May 1982.

In 1983, the Social Security Amendments of 1983 (P.L. 98-21) required that new and replacement Social Security cards issued after October 30 be made of banknote paper and, to the maximum extent practicable, not be subject to counterfeiting.

In 1983, the Interest and Dividend Tax Compliance Act (P.L. 98-67) required social security numbers for all interest-bearing accounts and provided a penalty of $50 for all individuals who fail to furnish a correct taxpayer identification number—usually the social security number.

In 1984, the Deficit Reduction Act of 1984 (P.L. 98-369): (i) amended the Social Security Act to establish an income and eligibility verification system involving State agencies administering the AFDC, Medicaid, unemployment compensation, the food stamp programs, and State programs under a plan approved under title I, X, XIV, or XVI of the Act and permitted states to require the social security number as a condition of eligibility for benefits under any of these programs; (ii) amended Section 60501 of the IRC to require that persons engaged in a trade or business file a report with the IRS, including social security numbers, for cash transactions over $10,000; and (iii) amended Section 215 of the IRC to authorize the Secretary of Health and Human Services to publish regulations that require a spouse paying alimony to furnish the IRS with the taxpayer identification number—i.e., the social security number—of the spouse receiving alimony payments.

In 1986, the Immigration Reform and Control Act of 1986 (P.L. 99-603): (i) required the Comptroller General to investigate technological changes that could reduce the potential for counterfeiting Social Security cards; (ii) provided that the Social Security card may be used to establish the eligibility of a prospective employee for employment; and (iii) required the Secretary of Health and Human Services to undertake a study of the feasibility and costs of establishing a social security number verification system.

In 1986, the Tax Reform Act of 1986 (P.L. 99-514) required individuals filing a tax return due after December 31, 1987 to include the taxpayer identification number—usually the social security number—of each dependent age 5 or older.

In 1986, the Commercial Motor Vehicle Safety Act of 1986 (P.L. 99-750) authorized the Secretary of Transportation to require the use of the social security number on commercial motor vehicle operators' licenses.

In 1986, the Higher Education Amendments of 1986 (P.L. 99-498) required that student loan applicants submit their social security number as a condition of eligibility.

In 1987, the SSA initiated a demonstration project on August 17th in the State of New Mexico enabling parents to obtain social security numbers for their newborn infants automatically when the infant's birth is registered by the State. The program was expanded nationwide in 1989. Currently, all 50

States participate in the program, as well as Washington, D.C., and Puerto Rico.

In 1988, the Housing and Community Development Act of 1987 (P.L. 100-242) authorized the Secretary of HUD to require disclosure of a person's social security number as a condition of eligibility for any HUD program.

In 1988, under The Family Support Act of 1988 (P.L. 100-485): (i) Section 125 required, beginning November 1, 1990, a State to obtain the social security numbers of the parents when issuing a birth certificate; and (ii) Section 704(a) required individuals filing a tax return due after December 31, 1989 to include the taxpayer identification number—usually the social security number—of each dependent age 2 or older.

In 1988, The Technical and Miscellaneous Revenue Act of 1988 (P.L. 100-647): (i) authorized a State and/or any blood donation facility to use social security numbers to identify blood donors (205(c)(2)(F)); and (ii) required that all Title II beneficiaries either have or have applied for a social security number in order to receive benefits. This provision became effective with dates of initial entitlement of June 1989 or later. Beneficiaries who refused enumeration were entitled but placed in suspense.

In 1988, the Anti-Drug Abuse Act of 1988 (P.L. 100-690) deleted the $5,000 and $25,000 upper limits on fines that can be imposed for violations of section 208 of the Social Security Act. The general limit of $250,000 for felonies in the U.S. Code now applied to social security number violations under section 208 of the Social Security Act.

In 1989, the Omnibus Budget Reconciliation Act of 1989 (P.L. 101-239) required that the National Student Loan Data System include, among other things, the names and social security numbers of borrowers.

In 1989, the Child Nutrition and WIC Reauthorization Act of 1989 (P.L. 101-147) required the member of the household who applies for the school lunch program to provide the social security number of the parent of the child for whom the application is made.

In 1990, under the Omnibus Budget Reconciliation Act of 1990 (P.L. 101-508): (i) Section 7201 (Computer Matching and Privacy Protection Amendments of 1990) provided that no adverse action may be taken against an individual receiving benefits as a result of a matching program without verification of the information or notification of the individual regarding the findings with time to contest; (ii) Section 8053, required a social security number for eligibility for benefits from the Department of Veterans Affairs (DVA); and (iii) Section 11112 required that individuals filing a tax return due after December 31, 1991, include the taxpayer identification number—usually the social security number—of each dependent age 1 or older.

In 1990, under the Food and Agricultural Resources Act of 1990 (P.L. 101-624), Section 1735: (i) required a social security number for the officers of food and retail stores that redeem food stamps; and (ii) provided that social security numbers maintained as a result of any law enacted on or after October 1, 1990, will be confidential and may not be disclosed.

In 1994, under the Social Security Independence and Program Improvements Act of 1994 (P.L. 103-296): (i) Section 304 authorized the use of the social security number for jury selection; (ii) Section 314 authorized cross-matching of social security numbers and Employer Identification Numbers maintained by the Department of Agriculture with other Federal agencies for the purpose of investigating both food stamp fraud and violations of other Federal laws; and (iii) Section 318 authorized the use of the social security number by the Department of Labor in administration of Federal workers' compensation laws.

In 1996, under the Personal Responsibility and Work Opportunity Reconciliation Act of 1996 (P.L. 104-193) (Welfare Reform): (i) Section 111 required the Commissioner of Social Security to develop and submit to Congress a prototype of a counterfeit-resistant Social Security card that: is made of durable, tamper-resistant material (e.g., plastic); employs technologies that provide security features (e.g., magnetic strip); and provides individuals with reliable proof of citizenship or legal resident alien status; (ii) Section 111 also required the Commissioner of Social Security to study and report to Congress on different methods of improving the Social Security card application process, including evaluation of the cost and workload implications of issuing a counterfeit-resistant Social Security card for all individuals and evaluation of the feasibility and cost implications of imposing a user fee for replacement cards; (iii) Section 316 required Health and Human Services to transmit to the SSA, for verification purposes, certain information about individuals and employers maintained under the Federal Parent Locator Service in an automated directory. The SSA is required to verify the accuracy of, correct, or supply to the extent possible, and report to Health and Human Services the name, social security number, and birth date of individuals and the employer identification number of employers. The SSA is to be reimbursed by Health and Human Services for the cost of this verification service. This section also required all Federal agencies, including the SSA, to report quarterly the name and social security number of each employee and the wages paid to the employee during the previous quarter; (iv)

Section 317 provided that State child support enforcement procedures require the social security number of any applicant for a professional license, commercial driver's license, occupational license, or marriage license be recorded on the application. The social security number of any person subject to a divorce decree, support order, or paternity determination or acknowledgement would have to be placed in the pertinent records, and social security numbers are required on death certificates; and (v) Section 451 provides that, in order to be eligible for the Earned Income Tax Credit, an individual must include on his or her tax return a social security number which was not assigned solely for non-work purposes.

In 1997, under the Department of Defense Appropriations Act of 1997 (P.L. 104-208—Division C—Illegal Immigration Reform and Immigrant Responsibility Act of 1996): (i) Sections 401–404 provide for 3 specific employment verification pilot programs in which employers would voluntarily participate. In general, the pilot programs would allow an employer to confirm the identity and employment eligibility of the individual. The SSA and the Immigration and Naturalization Service (INS) would provide a secondary verification process to confirm the validity of the information provided. The SSA would compare the name and social security number provided and advise whether the name and number match SSA records and whether the social security number is valid for employment; (ii) Section 414 required the Commissioner to report to Congress every year, the aggregate number of social security numbers issued to noncitizens not authorized to work, but under which earnings were reported. This section also required the Commissioner to transmit to the Attorney General a report on the extent to which social security numbers and Social Security cards are used by noncitizens for fraudulent purposes; (iii) Section 415 authorized the Attorney General to require any noncitizen to provide his or her social security number for purposes of inclusion in any record maintained by the Attorney General or INS; (iv) Section 656 provided for improvements in identification-related documents; i.e., birth certificates and driver's licenses. These sections require publication of regulations which set standards, including security features and, in the case of driver's licenses, require that a social security number appear on the license. Federal agencies are precluded from accepting as proof of identity, documents which do not meet the regulatory standards; and (v) Section 657 provided for the development of a prototype Social Security card.

In 1997, under the Taxpayer Relief Act of 1997 (P.L. 105–34), Section 1090 required an applicant for a social security number under age 18 to provide evidence of his or her parents' names and social security numbers in addition to required evidence of age, identity, and citizenship.

In 1998, under The Omnibus Consolidated and Emergency Supplemental Appropriations Act of 1999 (P.L. 105-277): (i) Section 362 provides that no funds appropriated for the Department of Transportation (DOT) may be used to issue the final regulations required by Section 656(b) of the Illegal Immigration Reform and Responsibility Act of 1996; and (ii) Section 656(b) prohibits Federal agencies from accepting as proof of identification a drivers license that does not meet standards promulgated by the DOT. The standards include a document that contains a social security number that can be read electronically or visually and is in a form that includes security features to limit tampering and counterfeiting.

In 1998, the Identity Theft and Assumption Deterrence Act of 1998 (P.L. 105-318): (i) made identity theft—i.e., transferring or using another person's means of identification—a crime, subject to penalties. "Means of identification" includes another person's name, social security number, date of birth, official State or government issued driver's license or identification number, alien registration number, government passport number, and employer or taxpayer identification number; and (ii) established the Federal Trade Commission as a clearinghouse to receive complaints, provide informational materials to victims, and refer complaints to appropriate entities, which may include credit bureaus or law enforcement agencies.

In 1998, Vice President Gore announced a new policy to allow victims of domestic violence to change their social security number without proof that the abuser had misused their social security number.

In 1998, P.L. 105-379 amended the Food Stamp Act, effective June 1, 2000, to require: (i) each State agency that administers the food stamp program to enter into a cooperative arrangement with the Commissioner of Social Security under section 205(r) of the Social Security Act to verify whether food stamp recipients are deceased to ensure that benefits are not issued to deceased individuals; and (ii) the Secretary of Agriculture to report to Congress and to the Secretary of the Treasury on the progress and effectiveness of the cooperative arrangements established.

CHAPTER 3:

SOCIAL SECURITY FUNDING

In General

Employees and self-employed persons pay contributions, known as social security taxes, into the social security system during their working years. The amount of these taxes, which is determined by Congress, is a percentage of one's gross salary, up to a designated limit. As set forth below, this tax deduction is generally designated as "FICA" on the employee's payroll stub. The employer is also required to pay social security taxes based on the employee's gross salary.

Social Security taxes are used to pay for all Social Security benefits, including a portion of the Medicare insurance coverage. The money Social Security takes in generally exceeds the money it spends. The excess, called the "reserve," is pooled into special trust funds, known as the Social Security Trust Funds. The money in those trust funds is invested in Treasury bonds, which the government, by law, is required to pay back with interest.

The Federal Insurance Contributions Act (FICA)

Social Security payroll taxes are collected under the authority of the Federal Insurance Contributions Act (FICA), and generally referred to as *FICA taxes*. FICA was enacted following the Social Security Act of 1935.

In the original Act, the benefit provisions were contained in Title II and the taxing provisions were contained in Title VIII. The taxing provisions were contained in a separate Title for constitutional reasons. Under the 1939 amendments to Title VIII, the taxing provisions were removed from the Social Security Act and placed in the Internal Revenue Code (IRC). The new IRC section was then renamed the *Federal Insurance Contributions Act.*

This distinction was made because, although the payroll taxes collected for Social Security are indeed "taxes," they can also be characterized as "contributions" to the social insurance system. Thus, "FICA" now refers to the tax provisions of the Social Security Act, as contained in the Internal Revenue Code.

General Revenue Funding

Social Security was designed to differ from welfare in that it was intended to be a self-supporting system rather than a government-subsidized system. Social Security is based on employee contributions, with the government acting as fund administrator rather than payer. For the most part, general tax revenues have never been used to support the Social Security system, except for the limited circumstances described below.

A table setting forth the percentage of general revenue financing of Social Security is set forth at Appendix 5.

Military Personnel

Military service was not covered employment under the Social Security Act until 1957. Even though subsequently covered, a military salary is minimal compared to the private sector. Thus, a soldier's military earnings result in reduced social security benefits. In 1966, to address this disparity, Congress enacted legislation which granted military personnel special non-contributory wage credits for service before 1957, and special military wage credits to boost the amounts of credited contributions for service after 1956. These credits were paid out of general revenues as a subsidy to military personnel.

Prouty Benefits

In 1966, Congress also recognized that certain elderly individuals, who attained the age of 72 prior to 1968, had not been able to work long enough under the Social Security system to become eligible for benefits. These individuals were granted special Social Security benefits—known as "Special Age 72" or "Prouty" benefits—which were funded entirely by general revenues.

The Taxation of Social Security Benefits

As part of the 1983 Amendments, Social Security benefits became subject to federal income taxes for the first time. The funds generated by this new tax are returned to the Social Security Trust Funds from the general revenue.

Social Security Trust Funds

The first Federal Insurance Contributions Act (FICA) taxes were collected in January 1937. Special Trust Funds were created for these dedicated revenues, and benefits were paid from the monies in the Social Security Trust Funds. Over the years, more than $4.5 trillion has been paid into the Trust Funds, and more than $4.1 trillion has been paid out in benefits. The remainder is currently on reserve in the Trust Funds and will be used to pay future benefits.

There have been 11 years in which the Social Security program did not collect enough FICA taxes to pay the current year's benefits. During these years, Trust Fund bonds in the amount of about $24 billion made up the difference. In 1982, the Retirement Trust Fund borrowed some of the money from the Disability and Medicare Trust Funds. However, this money was fully repaid in 1986, and was the only time this type of "interfund borrowing" has occurred.

Benefit Distribution

From 1937 until 1940, Social Security paid benefits in the form of a single, lump-sum payment. The purpose of these one-time lump sum payments was to provide some "payback" to those people who contributed to the program but would not participate long enough to be vested for monthly benefits. The average lump-sum payment during this period was $58.06.

Under the 1935 law, monthly benefits were to begin in 1942. The period between 1937 and 1942 was intended to both build up the Trust Funds and to provide a minimum period for participation in order to qualify for monthly benefits.

The Personal Earnings and Benefit Estimate Statement

The Social Security Administration (SSA) will provide each individual, upon written request, with a *Personal Earnings And Benefit Estimate Statement*. When an individual approaches age 60, the SSA will send an earnings statement without a request from the individual.

The earnings statement contains a breakdown of all the wages reported under one's social security number, as well as estimates of future Social Security benefits. This knowledge can assist an individual in planning their financial future and assessing what additional financial needs one may have upon retirement.

In order to obtain an earnings record, one must submit a Request For Personal Earnings And Benefit Estimate Statement (SSA Form 7004). It takes approximately four to six weeks to receive a statement.

A copy of the Request for Earnings and Benefit Estimate Statement (SSA Form 7004) is set forth at Appendix 6.

One should check their Social Security earnings record at least once every three years. Errors in the earnings record are more likely to occur if the individual changes jobs frequently or has more than one employer. If there are any errors in the report, one should contact the Social Security Administration and provide proof of their actual earnings, such as their W-2 forms, pay stubs, and tax returns. You should also report to the SSA if an incorrect name or social security number appears on the earnings statement. The Social Security Administration's toll-free telephone number is 1-800-772-1213.

CHAPTER 4:

THE SOCIAL SECURITY RETIREMENT PENSION

In General

During an individual's working years, they are required to contribute to the Social Security system through FICA taxes. When that person retires, the Social Security Administration pays the retiree a monthly benefit. The system is designed to work like a pension plan. The majority of Social Security recipients—approximately 60%—receive Social Security retirement benefits due to retirement.

A table setting forth the number of social security retirement beneficiaries and amount of payments distributed (1937–1996) is set forth at Appendix 7.

Determining the Retirement Age

In 1889, Germany was the first nation to adopt an old-age social insurance program. Germany initially set age 70 as the retirement age but, in 1916, lowered that age to 65. When America moved to social insurance in 1935, the German system was still using age 65 as its retirement age. It is a long-held belief that this was a factor in determining 65 as America's designated retirement age.

However, according to the Committee on Economic Security (CES), America's decision instead stemmed from two sources: (i) the prevailing retirement ages in the few private pension systems in existence at the time and; (ii) the 30 state old-age pension systems then in operation, half of which used 65 as the retirement age. In addition, the federal Railroad Retirement System passed by Congress earlier in 1934 also used age 65 as its retirement age. Based on this information, the CES decided on 65 as the retirement age for Social Security purposes. This decision was also confirmed by the actuarial studies which showed that using age 65 produced a manageable system that could easily be made self-sustaining with only modest levels of payroll taxation.

Nevertheless, as life expectancy increases, and the baby boom generation reaches senior citizenship, Social Security has foreseen the need to increase the eligibility age of retirees in future years. For example, Americans aged 65 or older comprised only 6.7% of the population in 1930 whereas, as of 1990, this segment of the population has expanded to 31.9%.

A table setting forth the number of Americans age 65 or older (1880-1990) is set forth at Appendix 8, and a life expectancy table depicting the remaining years of life based on age as of 1996 is set forth at Appendix 9.

Life expectancy at birth in 1930 was only 58 for men and 62 for women. Thus, there was much concern that, based on one's life expectancy at that time, Social Security was designed so that people would work for many years paying social security taxes, but would not live long enough to collect benefits.

Nevertheless, although life expectancy at birth was indeed less than 65, life expectancy as measured after the attainment of adulthood demonstrated that most Americans could expect to live to age 65 once they survived childhood. There was a low life expectancy at birth in the early decades of the 20th century caused by high infant mortality. Obviously, someone who died as a child would never have worked and paid into Social Security. Thus, the actuarial tables demonstrated that a more appropriate measure is life expectancy after attainment of adulthood.

For example, in 1940, almost 54% of men could expect to live to age 65 if they survived to age 21, and men who attained age 65 could expect to collect Social Security benefits for almost 13 years. These numbers were even higher for women. As of 1990, over 80% of those who survived to age 21 could expect to live to age 65, and those who attained the age of 65 could expect to collect benefits for almost 20 years.

A table setting forth the percentage of the population surviving from age 21 to 65 (1940-1990) is set forth at Appendix 10.

A table setting forth the average remaining life expectancy of individuals who survive to age 65 (1940-1990) is set forth at Appendix 11.

Eligibility

As set forth above, the Social Security Administration has set age 65 as the retirement age for a person who was born before 1938 to receive full social security retirement benefits (known as "full retirement age"). Beginning in the year 2000, the age at which a person's full retirement benefits are payable will increase gradually to age 67. For example, those born in 1940 reach "full retirement age" at 65 and 6 months. Individuals born in 1950, reach full retirement age at 66. Anybody born in 1960 or later will not be eligible for full retirement benefits until age 67.

A table depicting the eligibility age for full social security benefits according to year of birth is set forth at Appendix 12.

There are additional eligibility requirements for Social Security. For example, you must have worked for a specified number of years before you are eligible to receive Social Security retirement benefits. The amount of your monthly Social Security benefits is calculated according to a specified formula based on your average earnings over those employment years. Your earnings are tracked according to your Social Security number, which you are required to have if you are working. In fact, the Internal Revenue Service requires that a Social Security number be shown on tax returns for all dependents over the age of one.

As you work and pay Social Security taxes, you earn Social Security "credits," up to a maximum of four credits per year. The amount of money you need to earn one credit goes up each year. Currently, most people need 40 credits to qualify for benefits. Retirement benefits are calculated on earnings during a lifetime of work. During your lifetime, you will probably earn more credits than you need to be eligible for Social Security. However, it is your income, not the number of credits you earn, that determines the amount of your benefit under the Social Security system. Years of high earnings will increase the amount of the benefit. Because benefit computations are based on a person's date of birth and complete work history, there are differences in amounts among recipients.

In most cases, Social Security retirement benefits do not begin the month the person reaches the age of eligibility. Benefits usually begin the following month. To receive retirement benefits, you must have attained the age of eligibility for the entire month. Nevertheless, the law provides that one "attains" their age the day before their birthday. Thus, individuals born on the 1st or 2nd day of the month will usually be eligible for benefits beginning the month of their birth.

Family Benefits

When an individual becomes eligible for retirement benefits, certain family members may also be entitled to receive benefits. However, there is a limit to the amount of money that can be paid to a family. If the total benefits payable to the retiree's spouse and children exceed this limit, their benefits will be reduced proportionately. Nevertheless, the retiree's benefit will not be affected.

As further discussed below, eligible family members may include: (i) a spouse age 62 or older; (ii) a spouse under age 62 if he or she is taking care of the retiree's child who is under age 16 or disabled; (iii) a former spouse; (iv) children up to age 18; (v) children age 18-19 if they are full-time elementary or secondary students; and (vi) children over age 18 if they are disabled.

Spousal Benefits

A spouse is entitled to Social Security even if he or she never worked. If the married couple is over age 65 when the retiree's benefits begin, the spouse may be entitled to receive an additional amount equal to 50 percent of the retiree's benefit. A spouse may begin collecting benefits prior to age 65 provided the retiree is receiving benefits. However, if the spouse begins collecting benefits before age 65, his or her benefit is permanently reduced by a percentage based on the number of months before he or she reaches age 65.

For example, a spouse who begins collecting benefits at age 65 would receive approximately 46 percent of the retiree's full retirement benefit. If that spouse begins collecting at age 63, the benefit amount would be reduced to approximately 42 percent, etc. Nevertheless, if the retiree's spouse is taking care of a child who is under the age of 16 or disabled and receiving Social Security benefits, the spouse is entitled to full benefits regardless of age.

If both spouses worked and are eligible for their own social security benefits, the SSA always pays the individual benefit first. However, if the individual's benefit as a spouse is higher than their retirement benefit, he or she will get a combination of benefits equaling the higher spouse benefit.

For example, if a husband qualifies for his own retirement benefit of $250 and a wife's benefit of $400, at age 65, he will receive his own $250 retirement benefit plus $150 from the wife's benefit for a total of $400. However, if he decides to take his own retirement benefit before reaching full retirement age, both benefit amounts will be reduced.

A divorced spouse is also entitled to receive benefits on a former mate's Social Security record if the marriage lasted at least 10 years. The divorced spouse must be age 62 or older and unmarried. If the spouse has been divorced at least two years, he or she can get benefits even if the worker is not yet retired. However, the worker must have enough credits to qualify for benefits and be age 62 or older. The amount of benefits a divorced spouse receives has no effect on the amount of benefits a current spouse may obtain.

Unmarried Children Benefit

When an individual retires, monthly Social Security payments may also be made to unmarried children under age 18, or age 19 if still in elementary or secondary school, or children age 18 or over who were severely disabled before age 22 and who continue to be disabled. Each eligible child generally receives up to one-half of the retiree's full benefit.

Applying for Retirement Benefits

The SSA advises people to apply for retirement benefits 3 months before they want their benefits to begin. Even if an individual does not intend to retire, he or she should still sign up for Medicare 3 months before reaching age 65.

An application for social security retirement benefits can be made by calling the SSA or by visiting one of the offices. The SSA's toll-free telephone number is 1-800-772-1213. People who are deaf or hard of hearing may call the SSA's toll- free "TTY" number, 1-800-325-0778.

The following information and original or certified copies of listed documents will be needed to process the application:

1. The applicant's Social Security number;

2. The applicant's birth certificate;

3. The applicant's W-2 forms or self-employment tax return for the last year;

4. The applicant's military discharge papers if he or she had military service;

5. The applicant's spouse's birth certificate and Social Security number if the spouse is applying for benefits;

6. The applicant's children's birth certificates and Social Security numbers, if applying for children's benefits;

7. Proof of U.S. citizenship or lawful alien status if the applicant—or the applicant's spouse or child if applying for their benefits—was not born in the U.S.; and

8. The name of the applicant's bank and account number so the benefits can be directly deposited into the account.

Right to Appeal and Representation

If the application for Social Security benefits is not approved, the individual can appeal that decision. An applicant has 60 days to submit a written request for reconsideration. The request should be sent to the local Social Security district office, and should state the reasons why he or she disagrees with the determination. Depending on the nature of the issue, either a case review, a formal conference or a hearing may follow.

If the applicant does not appeal the determination within 60 days, their options are limited unless they can show there was a good reason for filing late. Without such a showing, the applicant may be able to file a new application and seek retroactive collection of benefits, or try to reopen the claim by filing a petition with a judge who is specially designated to hear Social Security appeals.

The applicant also has the right to designate a representative to act on his or her behalf in dealing with the SSA by filing an Appointment of Representative (SSA Form 1696-U4). The representative must also accept the appointment by signing the form.

It is important to select an individual who is qualified to act in this capacity as he or she will have the authority to act on the applicant's behalf in most Social Security matters. Often, the appointee will be an attorney who is familiar with the Social Security system. However, although an applicant does not need a lawyer to represent them on appeal, there are lawyers available who handle these types of cases. In addition, most legal services organizations will provide a lawyer free of charge to those unable to afford one.

A directory of National Legal Services for the Elderly is set forth at Appendix 13.

Once an appointment of representative is made and filed with the SSA, the SSA will deal directly with that individual on all matters affecting the applicant's Social Security claim.

If the representative will not be charging a fee for their services, they must also sign the waiver of fee section on the SSA form. Representatives who intend to charge a fee must obtain approval from the SSA by filing a fee petition or fee agreement with the SSA.

A copy of the Appointment of Representative (SSA Form 1696-U4) is set forth at Appendix 14.

Retiring before Full Retirement Age

If you wish, you may retire before full retirement age and receive Social Security retirement benefits at a rate which is reduced a small percentage for each month before you reach that age. However, the earliest age you can start collecting benefits is 62. Benefits are reduced five-ninths of one percent for each month you are retired before age 65, up to a maximum of 20 percent for people who retire the month they reach 62.

For example, if you sign up for Social Security at 62 years of age, you will receive approximately 80% of your full retirement benefit. At 64 years of age, you will receive 93-1/3% of your full retirement benefit.

It is important to note that your benefit is permanently reduced if you elect to start receiving it earlier than your full retirement age. The advantage to early retirement is that you begin to receive benefits before full retirement age and thus receive them for a longer period of time.

Working beyond Retirement Age

Some senior citizens continue to work full-time beyond full retirement age, and do not sign up for Social Security. Delaying retirement can increase your Social Security benefit by increasing your average earnings and will earn you a special credit from the Social Security program. This credit takes the form of a designated percentage added to the retiree's Social Security benefit depending on year of birth.

These increases are added in automatically from the time the individual reaches full retirement age until he or she starts receiving benefits, or until age 70. For example, an individual born in 1943 or later will receive an additional 8 percent per year to their benefit for each year of delayed retirement beyond full retirement age.

A table depicting the percentage of increase in social security benefits for each year of delayed retirement beyond full retirement age according to year of birth is set forth at Appendix 15.

Individuals who return to work after they start receiving benefits may be able to receive a higher benefit based on those earnings. This is because Social Security automatically recomputes the benefit amount after the additional earnings are credited to the individual's earnings record.

Nevertheless, some individuals who continue to work after retirement age, while also receiving benefits, may have their social security benefits reduced or eliminated depending on their earnings. Currently, this provision only affects people under the age of 70, and the reduction only applies to earned income.

In 1998, the earnings limit was $9,120 for people under age 65, and $14,500 for people age 65 through 69. An individual can still receive their entire social security benefit provided their earnings do not exceed the designated limit. As set forth below, if the earnings exceed the designated limit, some or all of the social security benefit may be withheld. For individuals under age 65, the SSA deducts $1.00 in benefits for each $2.00 earned above

$9,120. For individuals age 65 through 69, the SSA will deduct $1.00 in benefits for each $3.00 earned above $14,500.

Individuals are required to report their earnings up to age 70. In the year a recipient reaches age 70, they are only responsible for reporting their earnings for the months before the month they reach age 70. A recipient does not have to report their earnings if they are 70 or older.

Social security retirement benefits are not affected by income you may earn as a result of investments or savings you have set aside to supplement your retirement income.

Proof of Benefits

Every year, the SSA sends recipients an SSA-1099 form showing how much they received in the past year. This form can be used as proof of the benefit amount. SSA also sends a notice when the benefit amount increases because of an annual cost of living raise.

Employment Pension Benefits

If an individual receives a retirement pension from their employment, and also paid social security taxes, their retirement pension will not affect their Social Security benefit. However, pensions from work that is not covered by Social Security—such as federal civil service employment and some state or local government systems—may reduce the amount of one's Social Security benefit.

Representative Payees

If a family member entitled to receive Social Security or SSI benefits is legally incompetent or otherwise mentally or physically incapable of managing his or her benefits, another individual may be designated by the SSA to receive that family member's social security benefits. The designated individual is known as a "representative payee."

Although a friend or custodial institution—e.g., a nursing home—can be designated as a representative payee, the SSA prefers to appoint relatives who are personally concerned for the beneficiary. The Social Security or SSI benefits are sent directly to the representative payee who must manage the funds for the personal care and well-being of the beneficiary, and pay the beneficiary's bills from the funds.

Any remaining funds do not belong to the representative payee, but must be saved for the benefit of the recipient. The representative payee is obligated to report certain changes in the beneficiary's circumstances that could affect their continuing eligibility to receive benefits.

The Cost of Living Allowance (COLA)

From 1940 until 1950 virtually no changes were made in the Social Security program. Payment amounts were fixed, and no major legislation was enacted. Because the program was still very new, and because it was financed by low levels of payroll taxation, the value of social security retirement benefits was very low.

In fact, until 1951, the average value of the welfare benefits received under the old-age assistance provisions of the Act were higher than the retirement benefits received under Social Security. More elderly Americans were receiving old-age assistance than were receiving Social Security.

To help relieve this problem, major amendments were enacted in 1950. These amendments increased benefits for existing beneficiaries for the first time and dramatically increased the value of the program to future beneficiaries. By February 1951, there were more Social Security retirees than welfare pensioners, and by August 1951, the average Social Security retirement benefit exceeded the average old-age assistance grant for the first time.

A second increase was legislated for September 1952. Together these two increases almost doubled the value of Social Security benefits for existing beneficiaries. From that point on, benefits were increased only when Congress enacted special legislation for that purpose.

The law was changed in 1972, effective 1975, to provide for annual cost-of-living allowances based on the annual increase in consumer prices. This cost of living allowance (COLA) is an automatic annual increase in social security benefits given to help offset the effects of inflation on fixed incomes. Beneficiaries no longer have to wait for a special enactment by Congress to receive a benefit increase.

The Social Security Administration announced that Social Security and SSI benefits will increase 1.3 percent in 1999 as a result of the annual cost-of-living adjustment. The increase will begin with benefits that Social Security beneficiaries receive for December 1998. Increased payments to SSI recipients will begin on December 31.

For Social Security beneficiaries, the average monthly benefit amount for all retired workers will rise from $770 to $780. The maximum federal SSI monthly payments to an individual will rise from $494 to $500. For a couple, the maximum federal SSI payment will rise from $741 to $751.

A table of social security cost of living allowance (COLA) increases (1950-1998) is set forth at Appendix 16.

Recent Statistics

In November 1998:

44,211,900 persons received Social Security benefits, an increase of 269,400 (0.6 percent) since November 1997. Sixty- two percent were retired workers (27,492,900); and 10.9 percent were nondisabled widows and widowers (4,802,000). When including disabled widows and widowers, widowed mothers and fathers, and parents, the total number of widows and widowers is 5,217,700.

5,589,900 beneficiaries were receiving payments on the basis of disability, including 4,683,500 disabled workers; 712,500 disabled adult children; and 193,900 disabled widows and widowers. In addition, 190,400 spouses and 1,386,500 minor and student children of disabled workers were receiving benefits.

Seventy-two percent of the total were aged 65 or older (31,960,500); and another 8.7 percent were age 62-64 (3,851,900). Another 6.7 percent were children under age 18 (2,964,800).

Benefit payments from Social Security Trust Funds were $31.3 billion—$27.3 billion for OASI and $4.0 billion for DI.

Average monthly benefits were $770 for retired workers, $724 for disabled workers, and $739 for nondisabled widows and widowers.

357,100 monthly benefits were awarded, including 136,800 for retired workers and 63,900 for disabled workers.

Awards from January 1998 to date were 3,591,400—1,535,400 for retired workers; 576,900 for disabled workers; and 1,479,200 to all dependents and survivors.

Benefit awards during calendar year 1997 totalled 3,866,000—1,718,600 for retired workers; 587,400 for disabled workers; and 1,559,900 for their spouses and children and for survivors.

CHAPTER 5:

SOCIAL SECURITY DISABILITY INSURANCE

In General

The Social Security Amendments of 1954 initiated a disability insurance program which provided the public with additional coverage against economic insecurity. At first, the program merely involved a disability "freeze" of a worker's Social Security record during the years when he or she was unable to work due to the disability. While this measure offered no cash benefits, it did prevent such periods of disability from reducing or wiping out retirement and survivor benefits.

On August 1, 1956, the Social Security Act was amended to provide benefits to disabled workers aged 50–65 and disabled adult children.

In September 1960, President Eisenhower signed a law amending the disability rules to permit payment of benefits to disabled workers of any age and to their dependents.

By 1960, 559,000 people were receiving disability benefits, with an average benefit payment of approximately $80 per month.

Eligibility for Social Security Disability Insurance Benefits (SSDIB)

If a person has to stop working at any time before age 65 due to health reasons, he or she may be eligible for Social Security Disability Insurance Benefits. A person is eligible for benefits if: (i) they meet the Social Security standard for disability; and (ii) they are deemed "insured" because they have worked the required number of quarters for a person their age and contributed to the Social Security system.

If the individual is deemed disabled, benefits may start as early as five months after he or she becomes disabled, and he or she may be entitled to retroactive benefits for up to one year, depending on how much time elapsed between the onset of the disability and application filing date.

Applying for Social Security Disability Benefits

An individual should apply for social security disability benefits as soon as they become disabled. Nevertheless, benefits will not begin until the sixth full month of disability. This waiting period begins with the first full month after the date the disability began.

An application for disability benefits can be made by calling the Social Security Administration at 1-800-772-1213. SSA representatives will make an appointment for the application to be taken over the telephone or at any local Social Security office. People who are deaf or hard of hearing may call the SSA toll-free "TTY" number, 1-800-325-0778.

The claims process for disability benefits is generally longer than for other types of Social Security benefits, from 60 to 90 days. This is because it takes longer to obtain medical information and to assess the nature of the disability in terms of one's ability to work. The applicant is advised to expedite this process by providing the original or certified copy of certain documents and information when he or she applies, including:

1. The applicant's Social Security number;

2. The applicant's birth certificate or other evidence of date of birth;

3. The applicant's military discharge papers, if he or she was in the military service;

4. The applicant's spouse's birth certificate and Social Security number if he or she is applying for benefits;

5. The applicant's children's birth certificates and Social Security numbers if they are applying for benefits;

6. The applicant's checking or savings account information, so their benefits can be directly deposited;

7. The names, addresses, and phone numbers of doctors, hospitals, clinics, and institutions that treated the applicant and the dates of treatment;

8. The names of all medications the applicant is taking;

9. The applicant's medical records from his or her doctors, therapists, hospitals, clinics, and caseworkers;

10. The applicant's laboratory and test results;

11. A summary of where the applicant worked in the past 15 years and the kind of work he or she performed;

12. A copy of the applicant's W-2 Form (Wage and Tax Statement), or if the applicant is self-employed, his or her federal tax return for the past year;

13. The dates of any prior marriages if the applicant's spouse is applying.

Determining Disability

Qualifying disabilities are usually determined by a state agency that handles health issues—generally known as a disability determination service—which must find that the individual is suffering from a physical or mental impairment that meets SSA criteria. This would include a determination as to whether the disability prevents the individual from participating in "any substantial gainful activity." In addition, the disability must have lasted a full year, or be expected to last a full year, or be expected to result in the individual's death within a year.

Some of the factors that determine whether the applicant suffers from a qualifying disability include:

1. Present Employment— If the disabled applicant is working, and his or her earnings average more than $500 a month, he or she generally cannot be considered disabled.

2. Severity of Condition—The applicant's impairments must interfere with basic work-related activities for the claim to be considered.

3. Disabling Impairment—The SSA will check to see if the applicant's condition is on the SSA list of disabling impairments. This list contains impairments for each of the major body systems that are so severe they automatically mean the applicant is disabled. If the applicant's condition is not on the list, the SSA must decide if it is of equal severity to an impairment on the list. If it is, the claim will be approved. If it is not, a further determination must be made.

4. Ability to Perform Prior Work—If the applicant's condition is severe, but not of the same or equal severity as an impairment on the SSA list, then the SSA must determine if the impairment interferes with the applicant's ability to do the work he or she did in the last 15 years. If it does not interfere, the claim will be denied. If it does, the claim will be given further consideration.

5. Ability to Work—If the applicant cannot do the work he or she did in the last 15 years, the SSA then determines whether the applicant can do any other type of work. The SSA considers the applicant's age, education, past work experience, and transferable skills, and reviews the job demands of occupations as determined by the Department of Labor. If the applicant cannot do any other kind of work, the claim will be approved. If the applicant can perform other types of work, the claim will be denied.

In order to assist in this determination, the SSA requires the applicant to complete a disability report detailing: (i) the type and extent of the applicant's disability; (ii) the affect the disability has had on the applicant's ability to work; (iii) information about the applicant's employment; (iv) information about the applicant's medical records; and (v) information about the applicant's education and training.

A copy of the Social Security Disability Report (SSA Form 3368) is set forth at Appendix 17.

CHAPTER 6:

SURVIVORS' BENEFITS

In General

When an eligible individual dies, social security benefits are payable to certain family members. These benefits are called *survivors' benefits*. To be eligible, the decedent must have worked during their life, paid social security taxes, and earned enough credits. The number of credits needed to be deemed eligible for survivors benefits depends on the age of the decedent.

The younger the person is when they die, the fewer credits needed for family members to be eligible for survivors benefits. Under a special rule, benefits can be paid to a surviving spouse and minor children even if the decedent does not have the number of credits needed. Under this rule, they may be eligible for benefits if the decedent had credit for one and one-half years of work in the three years prior to their death. In general, individuals earn a maximum of four credits per year, and forty credits are the maximum number needed to be eligible for all Social Security benefits.

Eligible Family Members

Eligible family members generally include the surviving spouse, children and dependent parents.

Surviving Spouse

A surviving spouse is eligible for full benefits at age 65 or older, or reduced benefits as early as age 60. If the surviving spouse is disabled, benefits may begin as early as age 50. However, the surviving spouse's benefits may be reduced if he or she also receives a pension from a job where Social Security taxes were not withheld.

A surviving spouse is eligible at any age if he or she cares for the decedent's child who is under 16 or disabled and receiving benefits on the decedent's Social Security record.

In addition, a surviving divorced spouse may be eligible for benefits provided the marriage lasted 10 years or more, or if he or she is caring for the decedent's child who is under 16 or disabled and receiving benefits on the decedent's Social Security record. However, the child must be the surviving divorced spouse's natural or legally adopted child. Benefits paid to a surviving divorced spouse who is age 60 or older, or age 50 to 60 if disabled, will not affect the benefit rates for other survivors who are receiving benefits.

When a surviving spouse who is receiving benefits remarries, the remarriage has no effect on the benefits being paid to the decedent's minor children. In addition, if the new spouse wishes to adopt children already entitled to survivor's benefits, the adoption does not terminate a child's benefits. However, if the surviving spouse is receiving benefits solely because he or she is caring for the decedent's minor children, those benefits would end at the time of remarriage unless the surviving spouse is age 60, or age 50 and disabled. If the surviving spouse marries someone who is also receiving Social Security benefits, he or she may get benefits on the new spouse's record at age 62 or older if those benefits are higher.

Unmarried Children

Unmarried children are eligible if they are either under the age of 18, or up to age 19 if they are attending elementary or secondary school full-time. A child can get benefits at any age if he or she was disabled before age 22 and remains disabled. Under certain circumstances, benefits may also be paid to stepchildren, grandchildren or adopted children.

Dependent Parents

Dependent parents are eligible for benefits at age 62 or older.

Applying for Survivors Benefits

It is important to apply for survivors benefits promptly because benefits are generally retroactive only up to 6 months. Application may be made by telephone or at any Social Security office. The following information and original or certified copies of listed documents will be needed to process the application:

    1. The decedent's social security number;

    2. The applicant's social security number;

    3. A marriage certificate if the applicant is a surviving spouse;

    4. The divorce papers if the applicant is a surviving divorced spouse;

    5. Dependent children's social security numbers;

    6. The decedent's W-2 forms or federal self- employment tax return for the most recent year; and

    7. The name of the applicant's bank and account number for direct deposit of benefits into the account.

However, if the surviving spouse has already been getting spousal benefits on the decedent's social security record when he or she dies, the surviving spouse need only report the death to the SSA and their existing benefits will be redesignated as survivors benefits.

If the spouse is already receiving benefits on his or her own social security record, he or she needs to apply for survivors benefits to see whether they are entitled to more benefits as a surviving spouse.

Benefits being received by children will automatically be redesignated as survivors benefits once the death is reported to the SSA.

Amount of Benefits

The amount of survivors benefits one's family members receive from Social Security depends on the decedent's average lifetime earnings. Of course, the higher the earnings, the higher the benefit amount. The amount is calculated as a percentage of the decedent's basic Social Security benefit. In general, the following percentages apply:

1. Surviving spouse age 65 or older—100 percent.
2. Surviving spouse age 60–64—Approximately 71 to 94 percent.
3. Surviving spouse, any age, with a child under age 16—75 percent.
4. Children—75 percent.

The amount of benefits may be reduced if the recipient's earnings exceed certain limits. However, those earnings would reduce only the working individual's survivors benefits and not the benefits of other family members.

Family Maximum

Each family member entitled to a monthly benefit will receive one. The total benefits received by the family, however, cannot exceed the family maximum amount. The limit varies, but is generally equal to approximately 150 to 180 percent of the decedent's benefit rate. That amount is divided among all entitled dependents. The more dependents who receive benefits on the worker's Social Security record, the lower the benefit amount will be for each dependent.

Special One-Time Payment

There is a special one-time payment—currently $255—that can be paid to a surviving spouse or minor child provided they meet certain requirements and the decedent had enough work credits at the time of death.

CHAPTER 7:

SUPPLEMENTAL SECURITY INCOME (SSI)

In General

In the 1970s, the Social Security Administration (SSA) became responsible for a new program known as Supplemental Security Income (SSI). The original Act of 1935 included programs for needy aged and blind individuals and, in 1950, needy disabled individuals were added. However, these three programs were known as the "adult categories" and were administered by state and local governments with partial Federal funding. Over the years, the state programs became more complex and payments were inconsistent among the states. For example, payments varied more than 300% from state to state.

In 1969, President Nixon identified a need to reform these programs and, in 1971, Secretary of Health, Education and Welfare, Elliot Richardson, proposed that the SSA assume responsibility for the "adult categories." In the 1972 Social Security Amendment, Congress federalized the "adult categories" by creating the SSI program and assigned responsibility for its administration to the SSA. The SSA was chosen to administer the new program because of its reputation for successful administration of the existing social insurance programs.

SSI is basically a federal welfare program for adults and children who are disabled or blind, and people aged 65 and over with low income and few financial resources. General tax revenues from the U.S. Treasury are used to finance the SSI program.

A table setting forth the number of SSI beneficiaries and amount of payments distributed (1974–1997) is set forth at Appendix 18.

Eligibility

In order to be eligible for SSI payments, one's income and assets must fall below certain established limits. Not all assets are taken into account. For example, a home and personal belongings are not counted, but bank accounts and cash on hand are included in the calculation. In addition, although eligibility for SSI would not be affected by the ability of one's children to support them, any support actually received from one's children would be considered income for SSI purposes and could affect the amount of your payment.

Although SSI is a federal program, some states supplement the national payments and have established higher SSI rates and allow higher income limits than others. It is important, therefore, to ascertain your individual state's eligibility for the SSI program. Unlike the income limits, however, the SSI asset limits do not vary among the states.

You don't have to qualify for Social Security benefits in order to get SSI, and it is possible to get both Social Security and SSI. However, if you're applying based on a disability, you must meet the same standard for disability as with regular Social Security benefits.

Benefits

The SSI program provides a basic payment for an eligible individual and a larger amount for an eligible couple. The payment for a couple is lower than that made to two individuals because married people living together generally share expenses and live more economically than two people living independently.

People who qualify for SSI receive a check each month. The amount of benefit may vary depending on the recipient's state of residence and level of income. If you qualify for SSI, you are also automatically entitled to health care coverage under the Medicaid program. In addition, an SSI recipient may also be eligible for food stamps and other social services.

One can apply for SSI and Medicaid by completing forms provided by their local welfare office, department of social services or SSA office. If the application is approved, the recipient will be paid benefits based on the date the application was filed.

The SSA reviews every SSI case from time to time to make sure the individuals who are receiving checks are still eligible and entitled to receive benefits. The review also determines if the individuals are receiving the correct amounts.

Right to Appeal and Representation

If the application for SSI benefits is not approved, the individual can appeal that decision. The procedure for appealing an SSI determination is similar to appealing for more Social Security benefits. An applicant has 60 days to submit a written request for reconsideration. The request should be sent to the local Social Security district office, and should state the reasons why he or she disagrees with the determination. Depending on the nature of the issue, either a case review, a formal conference or a hearing may follow.

If the applicant does not appeal the determination within 60 days, their options are limited unless they can show there was a good reason for filing late. Without such a showing, the applicant may be able to file a new application and seek retroactive collection of benefits, or try to reopen the claim by filing a petition with a judge who is specially designated to hear Social Security appeals.

The applicant also has the right to designate a representative to act on his or her behalf in dealing with the SSA by filing an Appointment of Representative form (SSA Form 1696-U4). The representative must also accept the appointment by signing the form.

It is important to select an individual who is qualified to act in this capacity as he or she will have the authority to act on the applicant's behalf in most Social Security matters. Often, the appointee will be an attorney who is familiar with the Social Security system. An applicant does not need a lawyer to represent them on appeal, however, there are lawyers available who handle these type of cases. In addition, most legal services organizations will provide a lawyer free of charge to those unable to afford one. Once an appointment of representative is made and filed with the SSA, the SSA will deal directly with that individual on all matters affecting the applicant's Social Security claim.

If the representative will not be charging a fee for their services, they must also sign the waiver of fee section on the SSA form. Representatives who intend to charge a fee must obtain approval from the SSA by filing a fee petition or fee agreement with the SSA.

A copy of the Appointment of Representative (SSA Form 1696-U4) is set forth at Appendix 14.

Recent Statistics

In 1998, fifty-five percent of SSI recipients were between the ages of 18 and 64; 31 percent were aged 65 or older; and 14 percent were under age 18.

Federally-administered payments in November 1998 totaled nearly $2.6 billion; over $2.3 billion in Federal SSI payments, and $264 million in State supplementation.

The average monthly federally-administered payment in November 1998 was $359—including $447 to recipients under age 18, $384 to those ages 18 to 64, and $281 to persons aged 65 or older.

Over 2.4 million SSI recipients (37 percent) also received Social Security benefits, including 61 percent of those aged 65 or older, and 26 percent of those under age 65.

The total number of persons receiving Social Security benefits, SSI, or both in November 1998 was 48,391,444.

CHAPTER 8:

MEDICARE AND SUPPLEMENTAL
HEALTH CARE COVERAGE

In General

Medicare is a federal health insurance program administered by the Social Security Administration (SSA), designated for seniors and people with disabilities, regardless of income. Medicare was passed into law on July 30, 1965 but beneficiaries were first able to sign-up for the program on July 1, 1966. Medicare is an entitlement program funded by payroll taxes. The Medicare program is administered by private health insurance companies who contract with the federal government to process claims.

Eligibility and Coverage

When a person reaches age 65, he or she usually becomes eligible for Medicare. Unfortunately, Medicare does not cover all health-related expenses, and it is wise to supplement Medicare with additional health insurance coverage.

For example, Medicare does not pay for dentures and routine dental care, eyeglasses, hearing aids, prescription drugs, routine physical checkups, orthopedic devices, and non-skilled nursing home care—items that account for a considerable portion of medical expenses, particularly for senior citizens.

As set forth below, there are two parts to the Medicare policy: (i) Part A Hospitalization Coverage; and (ii) Part B Medical Coverage.

Part A Hospitalization Coverage

Part A is hospital insurance that covers hospital care as well as skilled nursing facility, hospice and home health care. Under Part A, there is a designated deductible—i.e., an initial amount one must pay for their hospitalization before Medicare begins to pay any additional expenses. This amount—known as the hospital deductible—increases every January 1st. As of January 1, 1998, the hospital deductible amount was $764.

Medicare Part A benefits are free to most people 65 and older. In general, anyone eligible for Social Security or Railroad Retirement Benefits are also eligible for free Part A benefits. Persons who have been receiving Social Security disability benefits for a period of 24 months also qualify for Part A hospital coverage. Others may be eligible for Medicare if they pay a monthly premium.

If an individual has enrolled in Medicare and is also working and covered under their employer's group health plan, Medicare is still the primary payer if the employer has less than 20 employees. Medicare is the secondary payer if the employer has 20 or more employees and provides group health insurance. However, because Medicare Part A is free, an eligible individual should sign up for Part A once they are eligible, whether or not they have other insurance.

Eligible persons receive a health insurance card, known as a Medicare card, to claim their benefits. Persons already receiving Social Security automatically receive Medicare cards as part of their Social Security benefits.

Under Part A, the duration of care per benefit period is limited. A *benefit period* begins when the patient first enters a hospital or other facility, and ends after he or she has been discharged from the facility for a continuous period of at least 60 days from the date of discharge. This rule is simply a measurement device. There is no limit to the number of periods in which one may receive benefits. The benefit periods depend on the type of care received, as follows:

Hospital Care

Part A entitles the patient to 90 days of in-hospital care for each *benefit period*. There is a deductible for each benefit period. In addition, the patient has to pay a *co-insurance amount* for days 61 through 90. After the patient has exhausted their 90 days of coverage, Medicare will pay for an additional 60 days of care during the patient's lifetime. The patient will have to pay a portion during these "reserve" days. Additional coverage may be obtained through the purchase of a MediGap policy, which is further discussed below.

Hospitals cannot refuse patients on the ground that their health coverage is through Part A of Medicare. Remember, though, not all hospital stays or services are covered by Medicare. It is the hospital's responsibility to inform you if something is not covered.

Skilled Nursing Facility Benefits

Part A entitles the patient to 100 days of care in a Medicare-certified skilled nursing facility (SNF) per benefit period, provided: (i) the patient was hospitalized for at least three days during the 30 days prior to admission in the SNF and (ii) the patient needs and receives daily skilled services. Medicare defines "daily" as seven days a week of skilled nursing and five days a week of skilled therapy. Skilled nursing and therapy services include evaluation and management as well as observation and assessment of a patient's condition. Medicare pays for the first 20 days in full. For days 21 through 100, the patient pays a portion of the costs.

Home Health Care Benefits

Medicare Part A covers up to 35 hours a week of home health aide and *skilled nursing services* if a patient is homebound and requires skilled services on an *intermittent* basis. *Skilled nursing services* include the administration of medication, tube feedings, catheter changes and wound care. *Intermittent* usually means less than five days per week, but some people who receive home health care services up to seven days a week will be covered if the services are only needed for a finite and predictable amount of time. A patient can also qualify for up to 35 hours per week of home health aide services if they are homebound and need skilled physical, speech or occupational therapy.

To be covered, the patient must receive services from a Medicare-certified Home Health Agency (CHHA). Medicare home health coverage is available indefinitely so long as the patient remains homebound and continues to require skilled nursing services on an intermittent basis or skilled therapy services.

There is no prior hospitalization requirement and the benefit covers individuals with chronic illnesses as well as those who are acutely ill. The benefit is available at no cost to the patient, and there is no deductible or co-insurance required.

Hospice Benefits

Under Part A, hospice benefits are available to terminally ill patients. Medicare will cover 95 percent of the cost of hospice care, and the patient will have to pay the remaining five percent. Once the patient elects Medicare hospice benefits, he or she becomes ineligible to receive benefits for hospital care related to the terminal illness.

Part B Medical Coverage

Part B of the medicare policy covers most reasonable and necessary health-related expenses, other than hospitalization, including certain physician services, therapy services, outpatient hospital care, laboratory and diagnostic tests, supplies, durable medical equipment such as a wheelchair, and many other specified medical expenses not covered by Part A. Medicare sets approved charges for all of the medical services it covers.

Medicare does not cover many common health expenses, such as prescription drugs, routine checkups, vision and hearing care, custodial care, or dental care. It also does not cover experimental procedures.

In 1997, Congress passed a law which set forth new covered preventive care services at no extra cost, including: (i) yearly mammograms; (ii) pap smears including pelvic and breast examinations; (iii) colorectal cancer screening; (iv) bone mass measurement; (v) flu and pneumococcal pneumonia shots; and (vi) diabetes glucose monitoring and diabetes education for individuals with diabetes.

Anyone who is eligible for Part A hospital coverage is eligible for Part B medical coverage, however, Part B is not free. There is a monthly premium that increases every January 1st. As of January 1, 1998, that amount was $43.80.

Part B medical coverage, unlike Part A, is based on a calendar year, rather than on benefit periods. The Part B medical coverage yearly deductible is $100.00 dollars. After the deductible is paid, Medicare pays 80% percent of the approved reasonable charges for covered services for the balance of the year.

Unfortunately, many health care providers charge substantially more than Medicare's approved charge for their services, and the patient must pay for any charges that are above the approved Medicare rate. For example, there is no limit on what ambulance companies and durable medical equipment suppliers may charge. The Medicare-approved portion may represent only a small part of the total bill.

Some health care providers, however, "take assignment," which means that they agree to accept Medicare's approved charge as payment in full. Medicare pays 80% of the approved charge, and the patient pays the remaining twenty percent. The local Medicare carrier has a directory that lists all doctors and suppliers in a particular area who always take assignment. To limit the amount one pays for medical expenses, it is a good idea to obtain a copy of this directory and use it when choosing health care providers.

When doctors don't "take assignment," federal law limits the amount that they may charge Medicare patients to 15% above Medicare's approved charge. Some states, including Massachusetts, Minnesota, Rhode Island, Pennsylvania, Ohio, Connecticut, Vermont and New York, have even stricter limits.

If an individual waits to enroll in Part B until he or she is older than 65, their monthly premium may be higher, since Medicare imposes a ten percent premium penalty for every year enrollment is delayed. However, if an individual is working and covered under their employer's group health plan, they may delay enrolling without a penalty until seven months after retirement.

However, it may not be cost-effective to sign up for Part B if you are already covered under an employer group health plan. That's because you will have to pay Medicare's Part B monthly premium and annual deductible, and your returns will be limited. In addition, it may be wise to stay in your employer's health plan after retirement, if that is an option, since any new insurance plans, including Medigap, may exclude pre-existing health problems for up to six months.

Denial of Medicare Claims

Under Medicare Part A hospital coverage, if a Medicare claim is denied, the hospital or Medicare review board must inform the claimant in writing if their stay will not—or will no longer—be covered by Medicare. The denial notice will set forth the procedures to follow in order to have the denial reconsidered. Many such denials are overturned.

If, after reconsideration, the claimant is still not satisfied, there are further remedies for appealing the decision. A large number of appeals are successful.

Under Medicare Part B coverage, if a claim is denied, the claimant will receive an "Explanation of Medicare Benefits." The claimant then has six months to ask for the denial to be reconsidered and overturned. If the claim is again rejected, the claimant has an additional six months to request a hearing through their local Medicare carrier. If the claim is again denied, the claimant has 60 days to request a hearing before an administrative law judge.

Medicare + Choice

In 1997, Congress passed a law which made many changes in the Medicare program, including a new section known as *Medicare + Choice*, which creates new health plan options for Medicare recipients.

Under the new law, a Medicare recipient can decide to: (i) continue receiving Medicare benefits under the original Medicare plan, (ii) continue receiving Medicare benefits under the original Medicare plan supplemented by one of ten available Medigap insurance policies, as further discussed below; or (iii) change to a plan that gives them at least the same, and possibly more, benefits than under the original Medicare plan.

There are differences among the new health plans including: (i) the cost; (ii) the availability of extra benefits; and (iii) the participant's choice in using certain doctors, hospitals and other medical providers.

In order to be eligible for Medicare + Choice, a recipient must have Medicare Parts A and B, and not have permanent kidney failure. Nevertheless, no matter which health plan option one chooses, they are still in the Medicare program and are still entitled to all of the services Medicare covers.

A Medicare Patient's Statement of Rights is set forth at Appendix 19.

Additional health care options available under the Medicare + Choice program include:

Medicare Managed Care Plan

A Medicare managed care plan is a Medicare approved network of doctors, hospitals, and other health care providers that agrees to give care in return for a set monthly payment from Medicare. Some managed care plans may provide extra benefits, and some may charge the participant a premium.

A managed care plan may be any of the following: (i) A Health Maintenance Organization (HMO); (ii) Provider Sponsored Organization (PSO); (iii) Preferred Provider Organization (PPO); or (iv) a Health Maintenance Organization with a Point of Service Option (POS).

An HMO or PSO usually asks the participant to use only the doctors and hospitals in the plan's network. If so, there are little or no out-of-pocket cost for covered services. A PPO or POS usually lets the participant use doctors and hospitals outside of the plan for an extra out-of-pocket cost.

Private Fee-for-Service Plan (PFFS)

A private fee-for-service plan (PFFS) is a Medicare-approved private insurance plan. Medicare pays the plan a premium for Medicare-covered services. A PFFS Plan provides all Medicare benefits. A PFFS Plan is not the same as a Medigap policy.

The PFFS Plan, rather than Medicare, decides how much to pay for the covered services the participant receives. Providers may bill the participant more than the plan pays, up to a limit, and the participant must pay the difference. It is likely that the participant will pay a premium for a PFFS plan.

Medicare Medical Savings Account Plan (MSA)

A Medicare medical savings account plan (MSA) is a health insurance policy with a high yearly deductible. This is a test program for up to 390,000

Medicare beneficiaries. Medicare pays the premium for the Medicare MSA Plan and deposits money into a separate Medicare MSA established by the participant. The participant uses the money in the Medicare MSA to pay for medical expenses.

The participant can accumulate money in their Medicare MSA to pay for extra medical costs. The insurance policy has a high deductible and there are no limits on what providers can charge above what is paid by the Medicare MSA Plan. A participant can only enroll in a Medicare MSA Plan during the month of November, and must remain in the plan for a full year.

Further information about the Medicare + Choice program may be obtained from the State Health Insurance Assistance Program in an individual's area. The State Health Insurance Assistance Program will help an individual with Medicare questions or provide information about other available health care options.

A directory of State Health Insurance Assistance Programs is set forth at Appendix 20.

Supplemental Health Insurance Programs

Medigap Insurance

Medicare does not pay for all of an individual's medical expenses. Therefore, eligible Medicare recipients may also purchase supplemental coverage known as Medigap insurance. Medigap policies generally pay for medical-related expenses not reimbursed by Medicare, such as hospital deductibles and co-payments.

Medigap policies are designed to supplement Medicare and generally do not cover long-term care, although some policies do provide for skilled nursing home care and at-home recovery care. There are ten variations of Medigap plans available through private insurance companies. The basic benefits offered under all plans include:

1. Hospital co-insurance;

2. Full coverage for 365 additional hospital days to be used after exhaustion of Medicare hospital reserve days;

3. Twenty percent co-payment for physician and other Part B services; and

4. Three pints of blood.

There are a number of additional benefits available depending upon the plan you select. These benefits include:

1. Coverage of the Medicare hospital deductible;

2. Skilled nursing facility daily co-insurance;

3. Coverage of the Part B $100 deductible;

4. Eighty percent of emergency medical costs outside the U.S. during the first two months of a trip;

5. Payment to cover the difference when a doctor's fees are over the Medicare-approved charge;

6. At-home custodial care in addition to and in conjunction with Medicare-approved home care;

7. Some prescription drug coverage; and

8. Some preventive medical care coverage.

There are many services a Medigap plan will not cover. These include:

1. Custodial care—such as feeding, bathing and grooming—either at home or in a nursing home;

2. Long-term skilled care in a nursing home;

3. Unlimited prescription drugs;

4. Vision care;

5. Dental care; or

6. Private nurses.

In addition, if Medicare refuses to cover medical care because it is unreasonable and unnecessary or experimental, Medigap will not cover it either.

Once you select a Medigap policy, you have 30 days to review the plan and cancel it without penalty. You also are allowed to change or cancel your policy once a year, although in most states your insurer can reject your application for more comprehensive coverage. However, if you wish to downgrade your policy, you may do so.

If an individual does opt to enroll in a Medigap plan, it's usually best to do so during the six months following enrollment in Medicare Part B. During that period, insurance companies must let the insured sign up for the plan of their choice, without regard to health or age.

Further information concerning Medigap insurance policies may be obtained from the National Insurance Consumer Helpline at (800) 942-4242.

The Qualified Medicare Beneficiary Program

Persons who receive Medicare and have income and resources below a certain amount may be eligible for the Qualified Medicare Beneficiary (QMB) program. Under the QMB program, the State pays Medicare premiums, deductibles and coinsurance for persons who qualify for the program.

Medicaid

Medicaid is a government program designed to provide health services, including nursing home care, to persons who are financially eligible. Medicaid eligibility is determined by a number of factors, the most important of which is income level. Only certain classes of individuals are eligible for Medicaid, including: (i) elderly persons who, although eligible for Medicare, cannot afford it; (ii) disabled persons; (iii) pregnant women; and (iv) children from low-income households.

Each state formulates and administers its own Medicaid program, following federal government guidelines, through matching federal funds based on the state's per capita income. Within these guidelines, states have considerable freedom in managing their own Medicaid program, thus coverage varies from state-to-state. For example, individual states set the financial eligibility criteria for Medicaid in their jurisdiction, often well below federally established poverty levels.

Medicaid offers more comprehensive coverage than Medicare. However, the program's low reimbursement levels discourages private medical providers from participating in the program.

Medicaid pays for costs not covered by Medicare for elderly persons who qualify for Medicare but cannot afford the Part A hospital deductible or Part B premium. Nevertheless, Medicaid is generally not an alternative resource to most persons in need of long-term care because of the stringent restrictions. To be eligible for Medicaid, one must first exhaust all of their assets and savings—not including their home—a process known as "spending down."

An exception exists under the spouse impoverishment provisions of Medicare, which provide that the spouse of a person receiving long-term care in a nursing home is permitted to keep a certain dollar amount of assets and income, and still be eligible for Medicaid. However, the amount one is allowed to retain is still very modest.

Older Americans Act

Under the *Older Americans Act of 1965*, states are allocated federal funds for the purpose of setting up agencies designed to provide services to persons over the age of 60. Unfortunately, these services are limited in scope, subject to eligibility standards, and not available in all areas. Services provided under this statute may include home health care, adult day care, homemaker services, transportation, and meal delivery programs.

Social Services Block Grants (Title XX)

The Social Services Block Grants program, established under Title XX of the Social Security Act provides for allocation of federal funds to the states to assist low-income persons with non-medical daily living services, such as those provided under the Older Americans Act. These services are also not widely available and thus may not be an option for most persons.

Anyone over 65 who is eligible for Social Security or Railroad Retirement Benefits— a program similar to Social Security for railroad employees, their spouses and survivors—is automatically eligible. People with disabilities who have received Social Security Disability Income for at least 24 months and some people who are receiving regular dialysis or have received a kidney transplant because of kidney failure are also automatically eligible. U. S. citizens are automatically eligible as are permanent legal residents who have been continuously residing in the United States for at least five years, though they must file an application.

Long-Term Health Care

This section discusses the availability of an insurance policy to protect individuals in need of care over an extended period of time. Unlike acute care—short-term, recuperative care provided by a hospital—long-term care is the type of care given to persons who have become disabled or who suffer from a chronic illness.

Long-term care is often a concern for senior citizens. Although many senior citizens are able to live out their lives independently and in good health, many others have health care problems which render them infirm and dependent on others to help them with their daily activities.

In 1991, 7 million senior citizens were in need of long-term care. This number is expected to increase to almost 9 million by the year 2000. The majority of the cost of this care is borne by the patients and their families. This is particularly burdensome in the retirement years when most older persons are on fixed incomes.

Home care costs can range from $50 to $200 per day, depending on the level of care and the number of hours provided. The average cost of care in a nursing home is estimated at $25,000 per year and more, depending on the facility, the location, and the level of care provided. Nursing home care is rarely covered by private insurance. If a senior citizen doesn't qualify under the Medicare or Medicaid programs, he or she must finance their own care.

A directory of State Offices of Long-Term Care Ombudsman is set forth at Appendix 21.

Nursing Homes

The term nursing home generally refers to a residential facility that provides shelter and care for senior citizens who are unable to live independently. As set forth below, there are three types of nursing homes.

Personal Care Nursing Facility

Personal Care Nursing Facilities provide the senior citizen who does not need any special medical care with room and board and basic assistance with daily activities. Medicare and Medicaid generally does not pay for this type of long-term care.

Medicaid Nursing Facility

Medicaid Nursing Facilities provide the senior citizen with a limited range of skilled nursing care, rehabilitation services, and other necessary health-related care. Medicare does not pay for residence in such facilities, however Medicaid may reimburse the costs of such care provided a doctor certifies that the senior citizen is in need of this level of care. Further, the resident must meet certain financial guidelines to qualify for admission.

Medicare Skilled Nursing Facility (SNF)

Medicare Skilled Nursing Facilities provide the senior citizen with the most highly skilled nursing care available outside of a hospital setting, including many specialized services. Medicare pays up to 150 days per calendar year for residence at such a facility, provided your physician certifies that you are in need of such a high level of care.

Federal law guarantees nursing home residents certain rights, applicable whether it is a publicly or privately owned institution. These rights include, but are not limited to: (1) the right to be free from physical or mental harm or abuse; (2) the right to privacy; and (3) the right to choose your own physician and participate in your health care decisions.

Long-Term Health Care Insurance Policies

There are long-term care insurance policies available to individuals who want to plan ahead for the possibility of needing long-term care in the future. With the exception of the Medicaid program, which has limited eligibility, much of what is covered under long-term health care insurance is either not covered at all, or only partially covered under Medicare or private health insurance policies.

Responding to this need, a large number of insurance companies have stepped in to fill the gap, providing a variety of insurance policies covering long-term care. If one is considering purchasing such a policy, it would be prudent to review the benefits being offered by the various companies in order to choose the policy that best fits your needs.

Although long-term care insurance can be very helpful if it is ever needed, it can also be quite costly, ranging anywhere from $250 to over $2000 per year for the average senior citizen who is in good health. Before taking on this considerable expense, it would be wise to carefully assess one's individual situation and investigate all resources available from other programs. Some of the factors one should consider when assessing the need for long-term care insurance, include:

1. The individual's present financial situation and projected financial situation following retirement;

2. The individual's ability to afford long-term care insurance;

3. The programs the individual expects to be eligible for upon retirement and whether they will be able to meet his or her needs;

4. The likelihood that the individual will require long-term care in the future, based on his or her present health and family history; and

5. The alternative resources the individual expects to have if long-term care is needed, such as family and friends, and the availability of community-based services.

Since long-term care insurance is a fairly recent development, one must be very careful in selecting and evaluating the various policies available, and inquiring into the background and stability of the companies offering such insurance.

Every policy generally contains some restrictions and limitations, and some policies may not be available due to such factors as age and health. Carefully read all of the provisions of the policy before making your decision. If any of the provisions are unclear, seek professional assistance in understanding the policy. In general, the policy should be flexible enough to cover all levels of nursing home and home health care without undue restrictions, such as stipulations as to the facilities at which the individual can receive care. In addition, the policy should have a renewal guarantee.

Although the provisions, limitations and restrictions of long-term care insurance policies may vary, there are a number of typical provisions found in most policies. Some of these provisions are discussed below.

Coverage

Long-term care insurance policies typically cover nursing home care. Some policies cover all levels of nursing home care—skilled nursing care, intermediate care, and custodial care—while others may cover only a certain level of care, such as skilled nursing care. It is best to purchase a policy that covers all levels of nursing home care, since long-term skilled nursing care is not usually needed. It is more likely that a person will need a lesser level of nursing home care, such as custodial care, over an extended period of time. Also be aware of any limitations or prerequisites to such care.

Home health care is generally provided for in long-term care insurance policies. Again, however, one must be aware of any limitations on the availability of such care. For example, some policies may only provide home health care after hospitalization, which may not be necessary in every case even though the individual may be in need of home health care services. In addition, long-term care insurance may include coverage for such services as assistance with household chores, shopping, transportation and personal hygiene, as well as long-term skilled nursing care.

Benefits

Most policies pay only a preset daily benefit for nursing home care or home health care, and the difference between the amount covered by the insurance and the actual costs of care is borne by the insured. Some policies allow the insured to pay higher premiums in return for higher daily benefits. When considering inflation, one must be aware that in many cases the benefits payable under the policy will not be increased. Therefore, the individual will be responsible for any escalation in the costs of care due to inflation.

To avoid this problem, one must shop around for a policy that provides for benefit increases over time due to inflation. One must also be aware of any limits the policy places on the duration of care and the benefits payable under the policy. Generally, policies that provide for a longer duration of care and benefits will be more costly.

Policy Restrictions

Most long-term care policies contain various restrictions. For example, a restriction on preexisting conditions—conditions that existed prior to the policy's effective date—typically denies the insured any benefits connected with those specific health conditions for a designated waiting period after the effective date of the policy.

Another restriction that often appears in long-term care insurance policies is the waiting period, known as the elimination period, during which the policy does not pay benefits. For example, if a policy specifies that benefits for home health care will begin on the 21st day, that means the insured is responsible for payment out-of-pocket for the first 20 days of home health care. Lower cost policies may contain waiting periods that are considerably longer. In considering a policy's waiting periods, you must determine whether it is worth the higher premium to insure that you will receive benefits at the earliest possible date.

To obtain further information on all aspects of long-term care, one should contact their State Office of Aging or State Office of Long-Term Care Ombudsman. In addition, there are a number of national and state organizations and agencies which are dedicated to helping the elderly.

A directory of the State and National Offices of Aging is set forth at Appendix 22, and a directory of the National Organizations of the Elderly is set forth at Appendix 23.

APPENDICES

APPENDIX 1:

SOCIAL SECURITY ADMINISTRATION—
REGIONAL OFFICES

REGIONAL OFFICE	AREAS COVERED
ATLANTA (REGION 1)	Alabama, Florida, Georgia, Kentucky, Mississippi, North Carolina, South Carolina, Tennessee
BOSTON (REGION 2)	Connecticut, Maine, Massachusetts, New Hampshire, Rhode Island, Vermont
CHICAGO (REGION 3)	Illinois, Indiana, Michigan, Minnesota, Ohio, Wisconsin
DALLAS (REGION 4)	Arkansas, Louisiana, Oklahoma, New Mexico, Texas
DENVER (REGION 5)	Colorado, Montana, North Dakota, South Dakota, Utah, Wyoming
KANSAS CITY (REGION 6)	Iowa, Kansas, Missouri, Nebraska
NEW YORK (REGION 7)	New York, New Jersey, Puerto Rico, Virgin Islands
PHILADELPHIA (REGION 8)	Delaware, Maryland, Pennsylvania, Virginia, West Virginia, District of Columbia
SAN FRANCISCO (REGION 9)	Arizona, California, Hawaii, Nevada, American Samoa, Guam, Saipan
SEATTLE (REGION 10)	Alaska, Idaho, Oregon, Washington

Source: Social Security Administration.

APPENDIX 2:

TABLE OF TOTAL SOCIAL SECURITY NUMBERS ISSUED
(1936–1996)

YEAR	TOTAL SOCIAL SECURITY NUMBERS ISSUED (Thousands)
1936–1937	37,139
1938	6,304
1939	5,555
1940	5,227
1941	6,678
1942	7,637
1943	7,426
1944	4,537
1945	3,321
1946	3,022
1947	2,728
1948	2,720
1949	2,340
1950	2,891
1951	4,927
1952	4,363
1953	3,464
1954	2,743
1955	4,323
1956	4,376
1957	3,639
1958	2,920
1959	3,388
1960	3,415

YEAR	TOTAL SOCIAL SECURITY NUMBERS ISSUED (Thousands)
1961	3,370
1962	4,519
1963	8,617
1964	5,623
1965	6,131
1966	6,506
1967	5,920
1968	5,862
1969	6,289
1970	6,132
1971	6,401
1972	9,564
1973	10,038
1974	7,998
1975	8,164
1976	9,043
1977	7,724
1978	5,260
1979	5,213
1980	5,980
1981	5,581
1982	5,362
1983	6,699
1984	5,980
1985	5,720
1986	5,711
1987	11,621
1988	11,370

YEAR	TOTAL SOCIAL SECURITY NUMBERS ISSUED (Thousands)
1989	8,049
1990	9,054
1991	7,509
1992	6,819
1993	5,893
1994	5,816
1995	5,465
1996	5,533
TOTAL =	381,000,000

Source: Social Security Administration.

APPENDIX 3:

SOCIAL SECURITY AREA NUMBERS
BY GEOGRAPHIC REGION

AREA NUMBER	GEOGRAPHIC REGION
001–003	New Hampshire
004–007	Maine
008–009	Vermont
010–034	Massachusetts
035–039	Rhode Island
040–049	Connecticut
050–134	New York
135–158	New Jersey
159–211	Pennsylvania
212–220	Maryland
221–222	Delaware
223–231	Virginia
232–236	West Virginia
232, 237–246	North Carolina
247–251	South Carolina
252–260	Georgia
261–267	Florida

AREA NUMBER	GEOGRAPHIC REGION
268–302	Ohio
303–317	Indiana
318–361	Illinois
362–386	Michigan
387–399	Wisconsin
400–407	Kentucky
408–415	Tennessee
416–424	Alabama
425–428	Mississippi
429–432	Arkansas
433–439	Louisiana
440–448	Oklahoma
449–467	Texas
468–477	Minnesota
478–485	Iowa
486–500	Missouri
501–502	North Dakota
503–504	South Dakota
505–508	Nebraska
509–515	Kansas

AREA NUMBER	GEOGRAPHIC REGION
516–517	Montana
518–519	Idaho
520	Wyoming
521–524	Colorado
525	New Mexico
526–527	Arizona
528–529	Utah
530	Nevada
531–539	Washington
540–544	Oregon
545–573	alifornia
574	Alaska
575–576	Hawaii
577–579	District of Columbia
580	Virgin Islands
580–584	Puerto Rico
585	New Mexico
586	Guam
586	American Samoa
586	Philippine Islands

AREA NUMBER	GEOGRAPHIC REGION
586	Northern Mariana Islands
587–588	Mississippi
589–595	Florida
596–599	Puerto Rico
600–601	Arizona
602–626	California
627–645	Texas
646–647	Utah
648–649	New Mexico
650–653	Wisconsin
700–728	Railroad Retirement Board
750–751	Hawaii
752–755	Mississippi
756–763	Tennessee

Note: Table is current as of 5/97. Some numbers are shown more than once because they have either been transferred from one State to another or divided for use among certain geographic locations.

Source: Social Security Administration.

APPENDIX 4:

APPLICATION FOR A SOCIAL SECURITY CARD

SOCIAL SECURITY ADMINISTRATION
Application for a Social Security Card

Form Approved
OMB No. 0960-0066

1	**NAME** TO BE SHOWN ON CARD →	First	Full Middle Name	Last
	FULL NAME AT BIRTH IF OTHER THAN ABOVE →	First	Full Middle Name	Last
	OTHER NAMES USED →			

2	**MAILING ADDRESS** → Do Not Abbreviate	Street Address, Apt. No., PO Box, Rural Route No.		
		City	State	Zip Code

3 **CITIZENSHIP** (Check One) →
☐ U.S. Citizen ☐ Legal Alien Allowed To Work ☐ Legal Alien Not Allowed To Work ☐ Other (See Instructions On Page 1)

4 **SEX** → ☐ Male ☐ Female

5 **RACE/ETHNIC DESCRIPTION** (Check One Only—Voluntary) →
☐ Asian Asian-American or Pacific Islander ☐ Hispanic ☐ Black (Not Hispanic) ☐ North American Indian or Alaskan Native ☐ White (Not Hispanic)

6 **DATE OF BIRTH** Month, Day, Year

7 **PLACE OF BIRTH** (Do Not Abbreviate) City State or Foreign Country — Office Use Only — FCI

8 **A. MOTHER'S MAIDEN NAME** → First / Full Middle Name / Last Name At Her Birth

B. MOTHER'S SOCIAL SECURITY NUMBER → (Complete only if applying for a number for a child under age 18.) ☐☐☐-☐☐-☐☐☐☐

9 **A. FATHER'S NAME** → First / Full Middle Name / Last

B. FATHER'S SOCIAL SECURITY NUMBER → (Complete only if applying for a number for a child under age 18.) ☐☐☐-☐☐-☐☐☐☐

10 Has the applicant or anyone acting on his/her behalf ever filed for or received a Social Security number card before?

☐ Yes (If "yes", answer questions 11-13.) ☐ No (If "no", go on to question 14.) ☐ Don't Know (If "don't know", go on to question 14.)

11 Enter the Social Security number previously assigned to the person listed in item 1. → ☐☐☐-☐☐-☐☐☐☐

12 Enter the name shown on the most recent Social Security card issued for the person listed in item 1. → First / Middle / Last

13 Enter any different date of birth if used on an earlier application for a card. → Month, Day, Year

14 **TODAY'S DATE** Month, Day, Year

15 **DAYTIME PHONE NUMBER** ( ) Area Code Number

DELIBERATELY FURNISHING (OR CAUSING TO BE FURNISHED) FALSE INFORMATION ON THIS APPLICATION IS A CRIME PUNISHABLE BY FINE OR IMPRISONMENT, OR BOTH.

16 **YOUR SIGNATURE** ▶

17 **YOUR RELATIONSHIP TO THE PERSON IN ITEM 1 IS:**
☐ Self ☐ Natural or Adoptive Parent ☐ Legal Guardian ☐ Other (Specify)

DO NOT WRITE BELOW THIS LINE (FOR SSA USE ONLY)

NPN			DOC	NTI	CAN		ITV
PBC	EVI	EVA	EVC	PRA	NWR	DNR	UNIT

EVIDENCE SUBMITTED

SIGNATURE AND TITLE OF EMPLOYEE(S) REVIEWING EVIDENCE AND/OR CONDUCTING INTERVIEW

DATE

DCL — DATE

Form SS-5 (2-98) Destroy Prior Editions

APPENDIX 5:

GENERAL REVENUE FINANCING OF SOCIAL SECURITY
(1966-1996)

CALENDAR YEAR	AMOUNT (in millions)	PERCENTAGE OF TOTAL TRUST FUND INCOME
1966	94	.40
1967	94	.37
1968	414	1.45
1969	458	1.37
1970	465	1.25
1971	538	1.31
1972	526	1.15
1973	494	.90
1974	499	.80
1975	515	.76
1976	717	.95
1977	741	.90
1978	757	.82
1979	675	.63
1980	670	.55
1981	843	.59
1982	844	.57
1983	6,662	3.88
1984	105	.05
1985	3,220	1.58
1986	160	.07

CALENDAR YEAR	AMOUNT (in millions)	PERCENTAGE OF TOTAL TRUST FUND INCOME
1989	34	.01
1990	(-)2, 864	(-).90
1991	19	.005
1992	14	.004
1993	10	.002
1994	7	.001
1995	(-332)	(-).08
1996	7	.001

Source: Social Security Administration.

APPENDIX 6:

REQUEST FOR EARNINGS AND BENEFIT ESTIMATE STATEMENT

Form Approved
OMB No. 0960-0466

SP

Request for Earnings and Benefit Estimate Statement

☐ Please check this box if you want to get your statement in Spanish instead of English.

Please print or type your answers. When you have completed the form, fold it and mail it to us. (If you prefer to send your request using the Internet, contact us at http://www.ssa.gov)

1. Name shown on your Social Security card:

_____ _____
First Name   Middle Initial

_____
Last Name Only

2. Your Social Security number as shown on your card:

☐☐☐ – ☐☐ – ☐☐☐☐

3. Your date of birth (Mo.-Day-Yr.):

☐☐ – ☐☐ – ☐☐

4. Other Social Security numbers you have used:

☐☐☐ – ☐☐ – ☐☐☐☐
☐☐☐ – ☐☐ – ☐☐☐☐

5. Your sex: ☐ Male ☐ Female

For items 6 and 8 show only earnings covered by Social Security. Do NOT include wages from State, local or Federal Government employment that are NOT covered for Social Security or that are covered ONLY by Medicare.

6. Show your actual earnings (wages and/or net self-employment income) for last year and your estimated earnings for this year.

A. Last year's actual earnings: *(Dollars Only)*

$ ☐☐☐ , ☐☐☐ . 0 0

B. This year's estimated earnings: *(Dollars Only)*

$ ☐☐☐ , ☐☐☐ . 0 0

7. Show the age at which you plan to stop working.

☐☐ *(Show only one age)*

8. Below, show the average yearly amount (not your total future lifetime earnings) that you think you will earn between now and when you plan to stop working. Include performance or scheduled pay increases or bonuses, but not cost-of-living increases.

If you expect to earn significantly more or less in the future due to promotions, job changes, part-time work, or an absence from the work force, enter the amount that most closely reflects your future average yearly earnings.

If you don't expect any significant changes, show the same amount you are earning now (the amount in 6B).

Future average yearly earnings: *(Dollars Only)*

$ ☐☐☐ , ☐☐☐ . 0 0

9. Do you want us to send the statement:
   • To you? Enter your name and mailing address.
   • To someone else (your accountant, pension plan, etc.)? Enter your name with "c/o" and the name and address of that person or organization.

Name _____

Street Address (Include Apt. No., P.O. Box, or Rural Route)

_____
City   State   Zip Code

Notice:
I am asking for information about my own Social Security record or the record of a person I am authorized to represent. I understand that if I deliberately request information under false pretenses, I may be guilty of a Federal crime and could be fined and/or imprisoned. I authorize you to use a contractor to send the statement of earnings and benefit estimates to the person named in item 9.

▲

Please sign your name (Do Not Print)

_____
Date   (Area Code) Daytime Telephone No.

Form SSA-7004-SM Internet (6-98) Destroy prior editions

APPENDIX 7:

TABLE OF NUMBER OF SOCIAL SECURITY BENEFICIARIES AND PAYMENTS DISTRIBUTED (1937–1996)

YEAR	NUMBER OF SOCIAL SECURITY BENEFICIARIES	AMOUNTS PAID
1937	53,236*	$1,278,000
1938	213,670*	$10,478,000
1939	174,839*	$13,896,00
1940	222,000	$35,000,000
1950	3,477,000	$961,000,000
1960	14,845,000	$11,245,000,000
1970	26,229,000	$31,863,000,000
1980	35,585,000	$120,511,000,000
1990	39,832,000	$247,796,000,000
1995	43,387,000	$332,553,000,000
1996	43,736,000	$341,098,061,000

Note: Recipients of one-time lump-sum payments.

Source: Social Security Administration.

APPENDIX 8:

AMERICANS AGE 65 OR OLDER (1880-1990)

YEAR	NUMBER OF AMERICANS AGE 65 OR OLDER (in millions)
1880	1.7
1890	2.4
1900	3.0
1910	3.9
1920	4.9
1930	6.7
1940	9.0
1950	12.7
1960	17.2
1970	20.9
1980	26.1
1990	31.9

Source: Social Security Administration.

APPENDIX 9:

LIFE EXPECTANCY TABLES, REMAINING YEARS OF LIFE BASED ON AGE, ALL RACES, 1996

AGE	BOTH SEXES	MALE	FEMALE
0	76.1	73.0	79.0
1	75.6	72.6	78.6
5	71.7	68.7	74.7
10	66.8	63.8	69.7
15	61.9	58.9	64.8
20	57.1	54.2	59.9
25	52.4	49.6	55.1
30	47.7	44.9	50.2
35	43.0	40.4	45.4
40	38.4	35.9	40.7
45	33.9	31.5	36.0
50	29.4	27.1	31.5
55	25.2	23.0	27.1
60	21.2	19.2	22.9
65	17.5	15.7	18.9
70	14.1	12.5	15.3
75	11.1	9.8	11.9
80	8.3	7.3	8.9
85	6.1	5.4	6.4

Source: United States Department of Health.

APPENDIX 10:

PERCENTAGE OF POPULATION SURVIVING
FROM AGE 21 TO AGE 65 (1940–1990)

YEAR	MALE	FEMALE
1940	53.9	56.2
1950	60.1	63.7
1960	67.8	72.3
1970	60.6	65.5
1980	71.3	76.9
1990	80.9	83.6

Source: Social Security Administration.

APPENDIX 11:

AVERAGE REMAINING LIFE EXPECTANCY FOR INDIVIDUALS SURVIVING TO AGE 65 (1940-1990)

YEAR	MALE	FEMALE
1940	12.7	13.1
1950	13.2	13.8
1960	14.6	15.3
1970	14.7	16.2
1980	17.4	18.6
1990	19.1	19.6

Source: Social Security Administration.

APPENDIX 12:

ELIGIBILITY AGE FOR FULL SOCIAL SECURITY BENEFITS ACCORDING TO YEAR OF BIRTH

YEAR OF BIRTH	FULL RETIREMENT AGE
1937 or earlier	65
1938	65 and 2 months
1939	65 and 4 months
1940	65 and 6 months
1941	65 and 8 months
1942	65 and 10 months
1943–1954	66
1955	66 and 2 months
1956	66 and 4 months
1957	66 and 6 months
1958	66 and 8 months
1959	66 and 10 months
1960 and later	67

Source: Social Security Administration

APPENDIX 13:

DIRECTORY OF NATIONAL LEGAL SERVICES FOR THE ELDERLY

NAME	ADDRESS	TELEPHONE NUMBER
American Bar Association Commission on Legal Problems of the Elderly	1800 M Street N.W., Suite 200 Washington, DC 20036	202-331-2297
Center for Social Gerontology	117 No. 1st Street, Suite 204 Ann Arbor, MI 48104	313-665-1126
Legal Counsel for the Elderly	1909 K Street N.W. Washington, DC 20049	202-434-2170
Legal Services for the Elderly	132 W. 43rd Street, 3rd Floor New York, NY 10036	212-595-1340
Medicare Beneficiaries Defense Fund	1460 Broadway, 8th Floor, New York, NY 10036	212-869-3850
National Caucus and Center on Black Aged	1424 K Street, NW, Suite 500 Washington, DC 20005	202-637-8400
National Health Law Program	2639 S. La Cienega Blvd. Los Angeles, CA 90034	213-204-6010
National Health Law Program	2025 M Street N.W. Washington, DC 20036	202-887-5310
National Senior Citizens Law Center	1052 W. 6th Street, 7th Floor Los Angeles, CA 90017	213-482-3550
National Senior Citizens Law Center	2025 M Street N.W, Suite 400 Washington, DC 20036	202-887-5280

APPENDIX 14:

APPOINTMENT OF REPRESENTATIVE

Social Security Administration
Please read the back of the last copy before you complete this form.

Form Approved
OMB No. 0960-0527

Name (Claimant) (Print or Type)	Social Security Number
Wage Earner (If Different)	Social Security Number

Part I   **APPOINTMENT OF REPRESENTATIVE**

I appoint this person, _____ ,
(Name and Address)

to act as my representative in connection with my claim(s) or asserted right(s) under:

☐ Title II (RSDI)   ☐ Title XVI (SSI)   ☐ Title IV FMSHA (Black Lung)   ☐ Title XVIII (Medicare Coverage)

This person may, entirely in my place, make any request or give any notice; give or draw out evidence or information; get information; and receive any notice in connection with my pending claim(s) or asserted right(s).

☐   I am appointing, or I now have, more than one representative. My main representative is _____ .
(Name of Principal Representative)

Signature (Claimant)	Address
Telephone Number (with Area Code) ( )	Date

Part II   **ACCEPTANCE OF APPOINTMENT**

I, _____ , hereby accept the above appointment. I certify that I have not been suspended or prohibited from practice before the Social Security Administration; that I am not disqualified from representing the claimant as a current or former officer or employee of the United States; and that I will not charge or collect any fee for the representation, even if a third party will pay the fee, unless it has been approved in accordance with the laws and rules referred to on the reverse side of the representative's copy of this form. If I decide not to charge or collect a fee for the representation, I will notify the Social Security Administration. (Completion of Part III satisfies this requirement.)

☐ I am an attorney.   ☐ I am not an attorney.   (Check one.)

Signature (Representative)	Address
Telephone Number (with Area Code) ( )	Date

Part III (Optional)   **WAIVER OF FEE**

I waive my right to charge and collect a fee under sections 206 and 1631(d)(2) of the Social Security Act. I release my client (the claimant) from any obligations, contractual or otherwise, which may be owed to me for services I have provided in connection with my client's claim(s) or asserted right(s).

Signature (Representative)	Date

Part IV (Optional)   **ATTORNEY'S WAIVER OF DIRECT PAYMENT**

I waive only my right to direct payment of a fee from the withheld past-due retirement, survivors, disability insurance or black lung benefits of my client (the claimant). I do not waive my right to request fee approval and to collect a fee directly from my client or a third party.

Signature (Attorney Representative)	Date

Form SSA-1696-U4 (4-95)   (See Important Information on Reverse)   FILE COPY
Use Until Stock Is Exhausted

APPENDIX 15:

PERCENTAGE OF INCREASE IN SOCIAL SECURITY BENEFITS FOR EACH YEAR OF DELAYED RETIREMENT BEYOND FULL RETIREMENT AGE

YEAR OF BIRTH	YEARLY RATE OF INCREASE (%)
1917-1924	3
1925-1926	3.5
1927-1928	4
1929-1930	4.5
1931-1932	5
1933-1934	5.5
1935-1936	6
1937-1938	6.5
1939-1940	7
1941-1942	7.5
1943 or later	8

Source: Social Security Administration.

APPENDIX 16:

SOCIAL SECURITY COST OF LIVING ALLOWANCE (COLA) INCREASES (1950–1998)

EFFECTIVE DATE	PERCENT INCREASE
9/50	77.0
9/52	12.5
9/54	13.0
1/59	7.0
1/65	7.0
2/68	13.0
1/70	15.0
1/71	10.0
9/72	20.0
3/74*	7.0
6/74	11.0
6/75	8.0
6/76	6.4
6/77	5.9
6/78	6.5
6/79	9.9
6/80	14.3
6/81	11.2
6/82	7.4
12/83	3.5
12/84	3.5
12/85	3.1
12/86	1.3
12/87	4.2
12/88	4.0

EFFECTIVE DATE	PERCENT INCREASE
12/89	4.7
12/90	5.4
12/91	3.7
12/92	3.0
12/93	2.6
12/94	2.8
12/95	2.6
12/96	2.9
12/97	2.1
12/98	1.3

Note: The increase in 3/74 was a special limited-duration increase. It was effective for only 3/74-5/74. In June 1974 all payment levels reverted to their 2/74 level and the 11% increase was permanently applied on this base.

Source: Social Security Administration.

APPENDIX 17:

SOCIAL SECURITY DISABILITY REPORT

SOCIAL SECURITY ADMINISTRATION

Form Approved
OMB No. 0960-0579

	For SSA Use Only Do not write in this box.
DISABILITY REPORT **ADULT**	Related SSN _____ Number Holder _____

SECTION 1 — INFORMATION ABOUT THE DISABLED PERSON

A. **NAME** *(First, Middle Initial, Last)*	B. **SOCIAL SECURITY NUMBER**

C. **DAYTIME TELEPHONE NUMBER** *(If you have no number where you can be reached, give us a daytime number where we can leave a message for you.)*

_____   _____   Your Number ☐   Message Number ☐   None ☐
Area Code   *Number*

D. Give the name of a **friend or relative** that we can contact (other than your doctors) **who knows about your illnesses, injuries or conditions** and can help you with your claim.

NAME _____   RELATIONSHIP _____

ADDRESS _____
        (Number, Street, Apt. No.(if any), P.O. Box, or Rural Route)

_____   _____   _____   DAYTIME _____   _____
City   *State*   *ZIP*   PHONE   *Area Code*   *Phone Number*

E. What is your **height** without shoes?   _____ _____   F. What is your **weight** without shoes?   _____
                          feet   *inches*   *pounds*

G. Do you have a **medical assistance card**? (For example, Medicaid or Medi-Cal)   YES ☐   NO ☐
If "YES," show the **number** here: _____

H. Can you **speak English**? YES ☐   NO ☐   If "NO," what languages can you speak? _____

If you **cannot speak English**, is there someone we may contact who speaks English and will give you messages? *(If this is the same person as in "D" above, show "SAME" here.)*

NAME _____   RELATIONSHIP _____

ADDRESS _____
        (Number, Street, Apt. No.(if any), P.O. Box, or Rural Route)

_____   _____   _____   DAYTIME _____   _____
City   *State*   *ZIP*   PHONE   *Area Code*   *Phone Number*

I. Can you **read English**? YES ☐   NO ☐   J. Can you **write more than your name in English?**   YES ☐   NO ☐

FORM SSA-3368-BK (7/98) DESTROY ALL PRIOR EDITIONS

PAGE 1

Disability Report - Adult - Form SSA-3368-BK

SECTION 2
YOUR ILLNESSES, INJURIES OR CONDITIONS AND HOW THEY AFFECT YOU

A. What are the **illnesses, injuries or conditions** that limit your ability to work? _____

_____

_____

B. How do your illnesses, injuries or conditions limit your ability to work? _____

_____

_____

_____

C. Do your illnesses, injuries or conditions cause you **pain**?   YES ☐   NO ☐

D. When did your illnesses, injuries or conditions
    first bother you?

Month	Day	Year

E. When did you become **unable to work** because of
    your illnesses, injuries or conditions?

Month	Day	Year

F. Have you **ever worked**?   YES ☐   NO ☐   *(If "NO," go to*
                                                                    Section 4.)

G. Did you **work at any time** after the date your
    illnesses, injuries or conditions first bothered you?   YES ☐   NO ☐

H. If "YES," did your illnesses, injuries or conditions cause you to: *(Check all that apply.)*

   ☐   **work fewer hours?** *(Explain below.)*
   ☐   **change your job duties?** *(Explain below.)*
   ☐   **make any job-related changes such as your attendance, help needed, or employers?**
       (Explain below.)

_____

_____

_____

_____

I. Are you **working now**?   YES ☐   NO ☐

    If "NO," when did **you stop working**?

Month	Day	Year

J. Why did you **stop working**? _____

_____

_____

SECTION 3—INFORMATION ABOUT YOUR WORK

A. List the **jobs** that you have had in the **last 15 years that you worked.**

JOB TITLE *(Example, Cook)*	TYPE OF BUSINESS *(Example, Restaurant)*	DATES WORKED *(month & year)*		HOURS PER DAY	DAYS PER WEEK	RATE OF PAY *(Per hour, day, week, month or year)*
		FROM	TO			
						$ /
						$ /
						$ /
						$ /
						$ /
						$ /
						$ /

B. Describe the **job above** that you did the **longest.** (What did you do all day in this job?)

_____

C. In **this job**, did you: Use machines, tools or equipment?   YES ☐   NO ☐
Use technical knowledge or skills?   YES ☐   NO ☐
Do any writing, complete reports, or perform
any duties like this?   YES ☐   NO ☐
Did you supervise other people?   YES ☐   NO ☐
If "YES," was this your main duty?   YES ☐   NO ☐

D. In **this job**, how many total hours each day did you:
Walk?   _____   Kneel? *(Bend legs to rest on knees.)*   _____
Stand? _____   Crouch? *(Bend legs & back down & forward.)* _____
Sit?   _____   Crawl? *(Move on hands & knees.)*   _____
Climb? _____   Handle, grab or grasp big objects?   _____
Stoop? *(Bend down and forward at waist.)* _____   Write, type or handle small objects?   _____

E. Lifting and Carrying *(Explain what you lifted, how far you carried it, and how often you did this.)*

_____

F. Check **heaviest** weight lifted:

☐ Less than 10 lbs.   ☐ 10 lbs.   ☐ 20 lbs.   ☐ 50 lbs.   ☐ 100 lbs. or more   ☐ Other_____

G. Check weight **frequently** lifted: *(By frequently, we mean from 1/3 to 2/3 of the workday.)*

☐ Less than 10 lbs.   ☐ 10 lbs.   ☐ 25 lbs.   ☐ 50 lbs. or more   ☐ Other_____

FORM **SSA-3368-BK** (7/98)

SECTION 4 — INFORMATION ABOUT YOUR MEDICAL RECORDS

A. Have you been seen by a **doctor/hospital/clinic** or anyone else for the illnesses, injuries or conditions that limit your ability to work?   YES ☐   NO ☐

B. Have you been seen by a **doctor/hospital/clinic** or anyone else for emotional or mental problems that limit your ability to work?   YES ☐   NO ☐

If you answered "NO" to both of these questions, go to Section 5.

C. List **other names** you have used on your medical records. ————————————————

Tell us who may have medical records or other
information about your illnesses, injuries or conditions.

D. List each DOCTOR/HMO/THERAPIST. Include your **next appointment**.

1.

NAME	DATES
STREET ADDRESS	FIRST VISIT
CITY STATE ZIP	LAST SEEN
PHONE _Area Code_ _Phone Number_ CHART/HMO #	NEXT APPOINTMENT
REASONS FOR VISITS	
WHAT TREATMENT WAS RECEIVED?	

2.

NAME	DATES
STREET ADDRESS	FIRST VISIT
CITY STATE ZIP	LAST SEEN
PHONE _Area Code_ _Phone Number_ CHART/HMO #	NEXT APPOINTMENT
REASONS FOR VISITS	
WHAT TREATMENT WAS RECEIVED?	

SECTION 4 — INFORMATION ABOUT YOUR MEDICAL RECORDS

DOCTOR/HMO/THERAPIST

3. NAME			DATES
STREET ADDRESS			FIRST VISIT
CITY	STATE	ZIP	LAST SEEN
PHONE	CHART/HMO #		NEXT APPOINTMENT
Area Code *Phone Number*			
REASONS FOR VISITS			
WHAT TREATMENT WAS RECEIVED?			

If you need more space, use Remarks, Section 9.

E. List each **HOSPITAL/CLINIC.** Include your **next appointment.**

1. HOSPITAL/CLINIC	TYPE OF VISIT		DATES	
NAME	☐ INPATIENT STAYS *(Stayed at least overnight)*		DATE IN	DATE OUT
STREET ADDRESS	☐ OUTPATIENT VISITS *(Sent home same day)*		DATE FIRST VISIT	DATE LAST VISIT
CITY STATE ZIP	☐ EMERGENCY ROOM VISITS		DATES OF VISITS	
PHONE				
Area Code *Phone Number*				

Next appointment _____ Your hospital/clinic **number** _____

Reasons for visits _____

_____

What **treatment** did you receive? _____

_____

What **doctors** do you see at this hospital/clinic on a regular basis? _____

_____

SECTION 4 — INFORMATION ABOUT YOUR MEDICAL RECORDS

HOSPITAL/CLINIC

2.

HOSPITAL/CLINIC	TYPE OF VISIT	DATES	
NAME	☐ **INPATIENT** STAYS *(Stayed at least overnight)*	DATE IN	DATE OUT
STREET ADDRESS	☐ **OUTPATIENT** VISITS *(Sent home same day)*	DATE FIRST VISIT	DATE LAST VISIT
CITY STATE ZIP	☐ **EMERGENCY ROOM** VISITS	DATES OF VISITS	
PHONE			
Area Code Phone Number			

Next **appointment** _____Your hospital/clinic **number** _____

Reasons for visits _____

_____

What **treatment** did you receive? _____

_____

What **doctors** do you see at this hospital/clinic on a regular basis? _____

_____

If you need more space, use Remarks, Section 9.

F. Does **anyone else have medical records or information** about your illnesses, injuries or conditions (Workers' Compensation, insurance companies, prisons, attorneys, welfare), or are you scheduled to see anyone else?

YES ☐   *(If "YES," complete information below.)*   NO ☐

NAME	DATES	
ADDRESS	FIRST VISIT	
	LAST SEEN	
PHONE	NEXT APPOINTMENT	
Area Code Phone Number		
CLAIM NUMBER *(If any)* _____		
REASONS FOR VISITS? _____		

If you need more space, use Remarks, Section 9.

SECTION 5 — MEDICATIONS

Do you currently take any **medications** for your illnesses, injuries or conditions?   YES ☐   NO ☐
If "YES," please tell us the following: *(Look at your medicine bottles, if necessary.)*

NAME OF MEDICINE	PRESCRIBED BY *(Name of Doctor)*	REASON FOR MEDICINE	SIDE EFFECTS YOU HAVE

If you need more space, use Remarks, Section 9.

SECTION 6 — TESTS

Have you had, or will you have, any **medical tests** for your illnesses, injuries or conditions?
YES ☐   NO ☐   If "YES," please tell us the following: *(Give approximate dates, if necessary.)*

KIND OF TEST	WHEN DONE, OR WHEN WILL IT BE DONE? *(Month, day, year)*	WHERE DONE? *(Name of Facility)*	WHO SENT YOU FOR THIS TEST?
EKG (HEART TEST)			
TREADMILL (EXERCISE TEST)			
CARDIAC CATHETERIZATION			
BIOPSY Name of body part_____			
HEARING TEST			
VISION TEST			
IQ TESTING			
EEG (BRAIN WAVE TEST)			
HIV TEST			
BLOOD TEST (NOT HIV)			
BREATHING TEST			
X-RAY Name of body part_____			
MRI/CT SCAN Name of body part_____			

If you have had other tests, list them in Remarks, Section 9.

FORM SSA-3368-BK (7/98)

SECTION 7 — EDUCATION/TRAINING INFORMATION

A. Circle the highest grade of **school** completed.

0   1   2   3   4   5   6   7   8   9   10   11   12   GED   College: 1   2   3   4 or more

Approximate **date** completed: _____

B. Did you attend **special education** classes?   YES ☐   NO ☐   If "YES,"

NAME OF SCHOOL _____

ADDRESS _____
(Number, Street, Apt. No.(if any), P.O. Box, or Rural Route)

_____
City   State   ZIP

DATES ATTENDED _____ TO _____

TYPE OF PROGRAM _____

C. Have you completed any type of **special job training, trade or vocational school?**   YES ☐   NO ☐

If "YES," what type? _____

Approximate date completed: _____

SECTION 8 — VOCATIONAL REHABILITATION INFORMATION

A. Have you received services from **Vocational Rehabilitation** or any other organization to help you get
back to work?   YES ☐   NO ☐   If "YES,"

NAME OF ORGANIZATION _____

NAME OF COUNSELOR _____

ADDRESS _____
(Number, Street, Apt. No.(if any), P.O. Box, or Rural Route)

_____
City   State   ZIP

DAYTIME PHONE NUMBER _____ _____
Area Code   Number

DATES SEEN _____ TO _____

TYPE OF SERVICES OR
TESTS PERFORMED _____
(IQ, vision, physicals, hearing, workshops, etc.)

B. Would you like to receive rehabilitation services that could help you get   YES ☐   NO ☐
back to work?

SECTION 9 — REMARKS

Use this section for any added information you did not show in earlier parts of this form. When you are done with this section (or if you don't have anything to add), be sure to go to the next page and complete the signature block.

SECTION 9 — REMARKS

_____
_____
_____
_____
_____
_____
_____
_____
_____
_____
_____
_____
_____
_____
_____
_____
_____
_____
_____
_____
_____

ANYONE MAKING A FALSE STATEMENT OR REPRESENTATION OF A MATERIAL FACT FOR USE IN DETERMINING A RIGHT TO PAYMENT UNDER THE SOCIAL SECURITY ACT COMMITS A CRIME PUNISHABLE UNDER FEDERAL LAW.

Signature of **claimant** or person filing on claimant's behalf _(Parent, guardian)_	Date _(Month, day, year)_

Witnesses are required **ONLY** if this statement has been signed by mark (X) above. If signed by mark (X), two witnesses to the signing who know the person making the statement must sign below giving their full addresses.

1. Signature of **Witness**	2. Signature of **Witness**
Address _(number and street, city, state, and ZIP code)_	**Address** _(number and street, city state, and ZIP code)_

FORM **SSA-3368-BK** (7/98)

APPENDIX 18:

TABLE OF NUMBER OF SSI BENEFICIARIES AND PAYMENTS DISTRIBUTED (1974-1997)

YEAR	NUMBER OF SSI BENEFICIARIES	AMOUNTS PAID
1974	3,249,000	$5,096,000,000
1975	4,360,000	$5,716,000,000
1980	4,194,000	$7,714,000,000
1985	4,200,000	$10,749,000,000
1990	4,888,000	$16,132,000,000
1995	6,514,000	$27,037,000,000
1996	6,613,000	$26,501,000,000
1997	6,495,000	$26,675,000,000

Source: Social Security Administration.

APPENDIX 19:

MEDICARE PATIENTS' STATEMENT OF RIGHTS

As a Medicare beneficiary, you have certain guaranteed rights. These rights protect you when you get health care; they assure you access to needed health care services; and they protect you against unethical practices. You have these Medicare rights whether you are in the Original Medicare Plan or another Medicare health plan. Your rights include:

1. The right to protection from discrimination in marketing and enrollment practices.

2. The right to information about what is covered and how much you have to pay.

3. The right to information about all treatment options available to you. You have the right to information about all your health care treatment options from your health care provider. Medicare forbids its health plans from making any rules that would stop a doctor from telling you everything you need to know about your health care, including treatment options. If you think your Medicare health plan may have kept your health care provider from telling you everything you need to know about your health care treatment options, you have a right to appeal.

4. The right to receive emergency care. If you have severe pain, an injury, sudden illness, or a suddenly worsening illness that you believe may cause your health serious danger without immediate care, you have the right to receive emergency care. You never need prior approval for emergency care, and you may receive emergency care anywhere in the United States.

5. The right to appeal decisions to deny or limit payment for medical care. If you are in the Original Medicare Plan, you have the right to appeal a denial of payment for a service you have been provided. Likewise, if you are enrolled in one of the other Medicare health plans, you have the right to appeal the plan's denial for a service to be provided. As a Medicare beneficiary, you always have the right to appeal these decisions.

6. The right to know how your Medicare health plan pays its doctors. If you request information on how a Medicare health plan pays its doctors, the plan must give it to you in writing. You also have the right to know whether your doctor has a financial interest in a health care facility, such as a laboratory, since it could affect the medical advice he or she gives you.

7. The right to choose a women's health specialist.

8. The right, if you have a complex or serious medical condition, to receive a treatment plan that includes direct access to a specialist.

If you believe that any of your rights have been violated, please call the State Health Insurance Assistance Program in your State.[1]

---

1   Source: Social Security Administration.

APPENDIX 20:

DIRECTORY OF STATE HEALTH INSURANCE ASSISTANCE PROGRAMS

STATE	TELEPHONE NUMBER
Alabama	1-800-243-5463
Alaska	1-800-478-6065
American Samoa	1-808-586-7299
Arizona	1-800-432-4040
Arkansas	1-800-852-5494
California	1-800-434-0222
Colorado	1-800-544-9181
Connecticut	1-800-994-9422
Delaware	1-800-336-9500
District of Columbia	1-800-336-9500
Florida	1-800-963-5337
Georgia	1-800-669-8387
Guam	1-808-586-7299
Hawaii	1-808-586-7299
Idaho	1-800-247-4422
Illinois	1-800-548-9034
Indiana	1-800-452-4800
Iowa	1-800-351-4664
Kansas	1-800-860-5260
Kentucky	1-800-372-2973
Louisiana	1-800-259-5301
Maine	1-800-750-5353
Maryland	1-800-243-3425
Massachusetts	1-800-882-2003

STATE	TELEPHONE NUMBER
Michigan	1-800-803-7174
Minnesota	1-800-333-2433
Mississippi	1-800-948-3090
Missouri	1-800-390-3330
Montana	1-800-332-2272
Nebraska	1-402-471-2201
Nevada	1-800-307-4444
New Hampshire	1-800-852-3388
New Jersey	1-800-792-8820
New Mexico	1-800-432-2080
New York	1-800-333-4114
North Carolina	1-800-443-9354
North Dakota	1-800-247-0560
Northern Mariana Islands	1-808-586-7299
Ohio	1-800-686-1578
Oklahoma	1-800-763-2828
Oregon	1-800-772-4134
Pennsylvania	1-800-783-7067
Puerto Rico	1-800-981-4355
Rhode Island	1-800-322-2880
South Carolina	1-800-868-9095
South Dakota	1-800-822-8804
Tennessee	1-800-525-2816
Texas	1-800-252-9240
Utah	1-800-439-3805
Vermont	1-800-642-5119
Virginia	1-800-522-3402

STATE	TELEPHONE NUMBER
Virgin Islands	1-800-778-6311
Washington	1-800-397-4422
West Virginia	1-800-642-9004
Wisconsin	1-800-242-1060
Wyoming	1-800-586-4398

Source: Social Security Administration.

APPENDIX 21:

DIRECTORY OF STATE OFFICES OF LONG-TERM CARE OMBUDSMAN

JURISDICTION	NAME	ADDRESS	TELEPHONE NUMBER
Alabama	Commission on Aging	136 Catoma Street, 2nd Floor Montgomery, AL 36130	205-242-5743
Alaska	Office of the Older Alaskans Ombudsman	3601 C Street, Suite 260, Anchorage, AK 99503	907-279-2232
Arizona	Aging and Adult Administration	1400 West Washington Street Phoenix, AZ 85005	602-542-4446
Arkansas	Arkansas State Office on Aging	1417 Donaghey Plaza South Little Rock, AR 72203	501-682-8952
California	Department of Aging	1600 K Street Sacramento, CA 95814	916-322-6681
Colorado	Aging and Adult Services Division	455 Sherman Street, Denver, CO 80203	303-722-0300
Connecticut	Department on Aging	175 Main Street Hartford, CT 06106	203-566-7770
Delaware	Division of Aging	1113 Church Avenue Milford, DE 19963	302-422-1386
District of Columbia	Office on Aging	1909 K Street N.W. Washington, DC 20049	202-833-6720
Florida	Program Office of Aging and Adult Services	154 Holland Avenue, Tallahassee, FL 32399	904-488-6190
Georgia	Office of Aging	878 Peachtree Street N.E. Room 632 Atlanta, GA 30309	404-894-5336
Hawaii	Executive Office on Aging	335 Merchant Street Room 241 Honolulu, HI 96813	808-548-2539
Idaho	Office on Aging	State House Room 114 Boise, ID 83720	208-334-3833

JURISDICTION	NAME	ADDRESS	TELEPHONE NUMBER
Illinois	Department on Aging	421 East Capitol Avenue Springfield, IL 62706	217-785-3140
Indiana	Department on Aging & Community Services	251 N. Illinois Street Indianapolis, IN 46204	317-232-7020
Iowa	Commission on Aging	914 Grand Avenue, Suite 236, Jewett Building Des Moines, IA 50319	515-281-5187
Kansas	Department of Aging	915 Southwest Harrison Topeka, KS 66612	913-296-4986
Kentucky	Division for Aging Services	275 East Main Street 6th Floor Frankfort, KY 40601	502-564-6930
Louisiana	Office of Elderly Affairs	4528 Bennington Avenue Baton Rouge, LA 70898	504-925-1700
Maine	Commission on Aging	State House Station No. 127 Augusta, ME 04333	207-289-3658
Maryland	Office on Aging	301 West Preston Street, Baltimore, MD 21201	310-225-1083
Massachusetts	Department of Elder Affairs	38 Chauncy Street Boston, MA 02111	617-727-7273
Michigan	Citizens for Better Care	1627 East Kalamazoo Lansing, MI 48912	517-482-1297
Minnesota	Office of Ombudsman for Older Minnesotans	444 Lafayette Road St. Paul, MN 55155	612-296-3969
Mississippi	Mississippi Council on Aging	421 West Pascagoula Street Jackson, MS 39203	601-949-2070
Missouri	Division on Aging	2701 West Main Street, Jefferson City, MO 65102	314-751-3082
Montana	Seniors' Office of Legal and Ombudsman Services, P.O.	P.O. Box 232 Capitol Station Helena, MT 59620	406-444-4676

JURISDICTION	NAME	ADDRESS	TELEPHONE NUMBER
Nebraska	Department on Aging	301 Centennial Mall South Lincoln, NE 68509	402-471-2306
Nevada	Division of Aging Services	340 North 11th Street Suite 114 Las Vegas, NV 89101	702-486-3545
New Hampshire	Division of Elderly and Adult Services	6 Hazen Drive Concord, NH 03301	603-271-4375
New Jersey	Office of the Ombudsman for the Institutionalized Elderly	28 West State Street Room 305 Trenton, NJ 08625	609-292-8016
New Mexico	State Agency on Aging	224 East Palace Avenue 4th Floor Santa Fe, NM 87501	505-827-7640
New York	Office for the Aging	Empire State Plaza Agency Building No. 2 Albany, NY 12223	518-474-7329
North Carolina	Division of Aging	693 Palmer Drive Raleigh, NC 27603	919-733-8400
North Dakota	Aging Services	State Capitol Building Bismarck, ND 58505	701-224-2577
Ohio	Department of Aging	50 West Broad Street 9th Floor Columbus, OH 43215	614-466-9927
Oklahoma	Special Unit on Aging	P.O. Box 25352 Oklahoma City, OK 73125	405-521-6734
Oregon	Office of Long-Term Care Ombudsman	2475 Lancaster Drive Building B, Number 9 Salem, OR 97310	503-378-6533
Pennsylvania	Department of Aging	231 State Street Harrisburg, PA 17120	717-783-7247
Rhode Island	Department of Elderly Affairs	160 Pine Street Providence, RI 02903	401-277-6883
South Carolina	Division of Ombudsman and Citizens' Service	1205 Pendleton Street Columbia, SC 29201	803-734-0457

JURISDICTION	NAME	ADDRESS	TELEPHONE NUMBER
South Dakota	Office of Adult Services and Aging	700 North Illinois Street Pierre, SD 57501	605-773-3656
Tennessee	Commission on Aging	706 Church Street Suite 201 Nashville, TN 37243	615-741-2056
Texas	Department on Aging	P.O. Box 12786 Capitol Station, Austin, TX 78741	512-444-2727
Utah	Division of Aging and Adult Services	120 North - 200 West Box 45500 Salt Lake City, UT 84145	801-538-3924
Vermont	Office on Aging	103 South Main Street Waterbury, VT 05676	02-241-2400
Virginia	Office on Aging	700 East Frannklin Street Richmond, VA 23219	804-225-2271
Washington	South King County Multi-Service Center	1200 S. 336 Street Federal Way Olympia, WA 98003	206-838-6810
West Virginia	Commission on Aging	State Capitol Charleston, WV 25305	304-558-3317
Wisconsin	Board on Aging and Long Term Care	214 North Hamilton Street Madison, WI 53703	608-266-8944
Wyoming	State Bar Association	900 8th Street Wheatland, WY 82201	307-322-5553

APPENDIX 22:

DIRECTORY OF STATE AND NATIONAL AGENCIES ON AGING

JURISDICTION	NAME	ADDRESS	TELEPHONE NUMBERS
Alabama	Commission on Aging	770 Washington Avenue Suite 470 Montgomery, AL 36130	(205) 242-5743, (800) 243 5463 (toll-free in state)
Alaska	Older Alaskans Commission	P.O. Box 110209 Juneau, AK 99811-0209	(907) 465-3250
Arizona	Aging and Adult Administration	1789 West Jefferson Site code 950-A Phoenix, AZ 85007	(602) 542-4446
Arkansas	Office of Aging and Adult Services	Department of Human Services P.O.Box 1437 Slot 1412 Little Rock, AR 72203	(501) 682-2441
California	California Department of Aging	1600 K Street Sacramento, CA 95814	(916) 322-5290
Colorado	Aging and Adult Services Division	Department of Social Services 1575 Sherman Street 4th floor Denver, CO 80203-1714	(303) 866-3851
Connecticut	Elderly Services	Department of Social Services 175 Main Street Hartford, CT 06106	(203) 556-3238, (800) 443-9946 (toll-free in state)
Delaware	Division of Aging	Department of Health and Social Services 1901 No. DuPont Highway New Castle, DE 19720	(302) 421-6791, (800) 223-9074 (nationwide toll-free)
District of Columbia	D.C. Office on Aging	441 Fourth Street, NW 1 Judiciary Square 9th floor Washington, DC 20001	(202) 724-5626

JURISDICTION	NAME	ADDRESS	TELEPHONE NUMBERS
Florida	Aging and Adult Services	1317 Winewood Blvd. Tallahassee, FL 32311-0700	(904) 488-8922
Georgia	Division of Aging Services	2 Peachtree Street 18th Floor, Atlanta	GA 30303
Hawaii	Executive Office on Aging	Office of the Governor 335 Merchant Street Suite 241 Honolulu, HI 96813	(808) 586- 0100
Idaho	Idaho Office on Aging	Statehouse Room 108 Boise ID 83720	(208) 334-3833
Illinois	Department on Aging	421 East Capitol Avenue, #100 Springfield, IL 62701-1789	(217) 785-2870, (800) 252-8966 (toll-free in state)
Indiana	Bureau of Aging and In-Home Services	P.O. Box 7083 Indianapolis, IN 46207-7083	(317) 232-7020, (800) 545-7763 (toll-free in state)
Iowa	Department of Elder Affairs	914 Grand Avenue Des Moines, IA 50319	(515) 281-5187, (800) 532-3213 (toll-free in state)
Kansas	Department on Aging	Docking State Office Building 915 Southwest Harrison Street Topeka, KS 66612-1500	(913) 296-4986, (800) 432-3535 (toll-free in state)
Kentucky	Division for Aging Services	275 East Main Street Frankfort, KY 40621	(502) 564-6930
Louisiana	Office of Elderly Affairs	P.O.Box 80374 Baton Rouge, LA 70898-0374	(504) 925-1700
Maine	Bureau of Elder and Adult Services	35 Anthony Ave Statehouse, Station 11 Augusta, ME 04333-0011	(207) 624-5335

JURISDICTION	NAME	ADDRESS	TELEPHONE NUMBERS
Maryland	Office on Aging	301 West Preston Street Baltimore, MD 21201	(410) 225-1100, (800) 243-3425 (toll-free in state)
Massachusetts	Executive Office of Elder Affairs	1 Ashburton Place Boston, MA 02108	(617) 727-7750
Michigan	Office of Services to the Aging	P.O. Box 30026 Lansing, MI 48909	(517) 373-8230
Minnesota	Minnesota Board on Aging	444 Lafayette Road St. Paul, MN 55155-3843	(612) 296-2770, (800) 882-6262 (toll- free nationwide)
Mississippi	Division of Aging and Adult Services	P.O Box 352 Jackson, MS 39205	(601) 359-4929, (800) 948-3090 (toll-free in state)
Missouri	Division of Aging	Department of Social Services P.O. Box 1337 Jefferson City, MO 65102-1337	(314) 751- 3082, (800) 392-0210 (toll-free in state)
Montana	Citizen's Advocate for Aging	Department of Family Services P.O. Box 80005 Helena, MT 59604	(406) 444-7786
Nebraska	Nebraska Department on Aging	301 Centennial Mall South P.O. Box 95044 Lincoln, NE 68509-5044	(402) 471-2306
Nevada	Division of Aging Services	Department of Human Resources 340 North 11th Street, Las Vegas, NV 89101	(702) 486-3545
New Hampshire	Division of Elderly and Adult Services	State Office Park South 115 Pleasant Street Annex #1 Concord, NH 03301-3843	(603) 271-4680, (800) 351-1888 (toll-free in state)

JURISDICTION	NAME	ADDRESS	TELEPHONE NUMBERS
New Jersey	Division on Aging	Department of Community Affairs, South Broad and Front Streets, CN 807 Trenton, NJ 08625-0807	(609) 292-4833, (800) 792-8820 (toll-free in state)
New Mexico	State Agency on Aging	228 East Palace Avenue Santa Fe, NM 87501	(505) 827-7640, (800) 432-2080 (toll- free in state)
New York	New York State Office for the Aging	Agency Building 2 Empire State Plaza Albany, NY 12223	(518) 474-4425
North Carolina	Division of Aging	Department of Human Resources 693 Palmer Drive Raleigh, NC 27603	(919) 733-3983 (800) 662-7030 (toll-free in state)
North Dakota	Aging Services Division	North Dakota Department of Human Services, P.O. Box 7070, Bismarck, ND 58507	(701) 224-2577 (800) 472-2622 (toll-free in state)
Ohio	Ohio Department of Aging	50 West Broad Street 9th floor Columbus, OH 43215	(614) 466-7246
Oklahoma	Aging Services Division	Department of Human Services, P.O. Box 25352, Oklahoma City, OK 73125	(405) 521-2327
Oregon	Senior and Disabled Services Division	Department of Human Resources Program Assistance Section 500 Summer Street NE, 2nd Floor, South Side, Salem, OR 97310-1015	(503) 945-5832 (800) 232-3020
Pennsylvania	Department of Aging	400 Market Street, Market Street State Office Building Harrisburg, PA 17101-2301	(717) 783-1550

JURISDICTION	NAME	ADDRESS	TELEPHONE NUMBERS
Rhode Island	Department of Elderly Affairs	160 Pine Street, Providence, RI 02903-3708	(401) 277-2858 (800) 322-2880 (toll-free in state)
South Carolina	Governor's Office: Division on Aging	202 Arbor Lake Drive Suite 301 Columbia, SC 29223	(803) 737-7500
South Dakota	Office of Adult Services and Aging	700 Governor's Drive Pierre, SD 57501	(605) 773-3656
Tennessee	Commission on Aging	500 Deadrick, Andrew Jackson Building, 9th Floor Nashville, TN 37243-0860	(615) 741-2056
Texas	Texas Department on Aging	P.O. Box 12786, Capitol Station Austin, TX 78711	(512) 444-2727, (800) 252-9240 (in state only)
Utah	Division of Aging and Adult Services	Department of Social Service, P.O. Box 45500, Salt Lake City, UT 84145	(801) 538-3910
Vermont	Department of Aging and Disabilities	103 South Main Street Waterbury, VT 056771-2301	(802) 241-2400
Virginia	Department for the Aging	700 East Franklin Richmond, VA 23219-2327	(804) 225-2271, (800) 552-4464 (toll-free in state)
Washington	Aging and Adult Services Adminstration	Department of Social and Health Services, PO Box 45050, Olympia, WA 98504-5050	(206) 586-3768, (800) 422-3263 (toll-free in state)
West Virginia	Commission on Aging	State Capitol Charleston, WV 25305	(304) 558-3317
Wisconsin	Bureau on Aging	Division of Community Services 217 South Hamilton Street, Suite 300 Madison, WI 53703	(608) 266-2536

JURISDICTION	NAME	ADDRESS	TELEPHONE NUMBERS
Wyoming	Division on Aging of Wyoming	Hathaway Building, Room 139 Cheyenne, WY 82002	(307) 777-7986, (800) 442- 2766 (toll-free in state)
National	National Association of State Units on Aging	1225 I Street NW Suite 725 Washington, D.C. 20005	(202) 898-2578
National	National Association of Area Agencies on Aging	1112 Sixteenth Street Washington, D.C. 20036	(202) 296-8130

APPENDIX 23:

DIRECTORY OF NATIONAL ORGANIZATIONS
FOR THE ELDERLY

NAME	ADDRESS	TELEPHONE NUMBER
American Association of Retired Persons	1909 K Street NW Washington, DC, 20049	202-872-4700
American Society of Aging	833 Market Street, Suite 516 San Francisco, CA 94103	415-543-2617
Choice in Dying	200 Varick Street New York, NY 10014	212- 366-5540
The Gerontological Society of America	1411 K Street NW, Suite 300 Washington, DC 20005	202-393-1411
Gray Panthers	311 S. Juniper Street, Suite 601 Philadelphia, PA 19107	215-545-6555
National Association of Area Agencies on Aging	600 Maryland Avenue SW West Wing, Suite 208 Washington, DC 20024	202-484-7520
National Association of Retired Federal Employees	1533 New Hampshire Avenue NW Washington, DC 20036	202-234-0832
National Association of State Units on Aging	600 Maryland Avenue SW Suite 208 Washington, DC 20024	202-484-7182
National Caucus and Center on Black Aged	1424 K Street, NW, Suite 500 Washington, DC 20005	202-637-8400
National Center on Rural Aging	600 Maryland Avenue SW West Wing, Suite 100 Washington, DC 20024	202-479-1200
National Citizens Coalition on Nursing Home Reform	1424 16th Street NW, Suite L2 Washington, DC 20036	202-797-0657
National Council of Senior Citizens	925 15th Street, NW Washington, DC 20005	203-347-8800
National Council on the Aging	600 Maryland Avenue SW West Wing, Suite 100 Washington, DC 20024	202-479-1200

NAME	ADDRESS	TELEPHONE NUMBER
National Indian Council on Aging	P.O. Box 2088 Albuquerque, NM 87103	505-242-9505
National Pacific/Asian Resource Center on Aging	2033 6th Avenue, Suite 410 Seattle, WA 98121	206-448-0313
Older Women's League	666 11th Street NW Lower Level B Washington, DC 20005	202-783-6686
Pension Rights Center	918 16th Street NW, Suite 704 Washington, DC 20006	202-296-3776
Society for the Right to Die	250 W. 57th Street New York, NY 10107	212-246-6973
Villers Foundation	1334 G Street NW Washington, DC 20005	202-628-3030

GLOSSARY

GLOSSARY

Asset - The entirety of a person's property, either real or personal.

Beneficiary - A person who is designated to receive property upon the death of another, such as the beneficiary of a life insurance policy, who receives the proceeds upon the death of the insured.

Death Benefit - The amount of money paid to the surviving spouse of a deceased Social Security beneficiary under certain circumstances.

Decedent - A deceased person.

Deductible - An amount an insured person must pay before they are entitled to recover money from the insurer, in connection with a loss or expense covered by an insurance policy.

Disability - Under the Social Security or Supplemental Security Income government programs, refers to the inability to do any substantial gainful activity because of a medically provable physical or mental impairment that is expected to result in death, or that has lasted, or is expected to last, at least 12 continuous months.

Earned Income - Income which is gained through one's labor and services, as opposed to investment income.

Indigent - A person who is financially destitute.

Life Expectancy - The period of time which a person is statistically expected to live, based on such factors as their present age and sex.

Long-Term Care - The services provided at home or in an institutionalized setting to older persons who require medical or personal care for an extended period of time.

Medicare - The program governed by the Social Security Administration to provide medical and hospital coverage to the aged or disabled.

Minor - A person who has not yet reached the age of legal competence, which is designated as 18 in most states.

Pension Benefits - An amount of money paid to an employee upon retirement based upon such factors as salary and length of employment.

Pension Plan - A retirement plan established by an employer for the payment of pension benefits to employees upon retirement.

Supplemental Security Income (SSI) - The government program awarding cash benefits to the needy, aged, blind or otherwise qualifying disabled.